Vocation
in Black and White

Vocation in Black and White

✦

Dominican Contemplative Nuns tell how God called them

Association of the Monasteries of Nuns of the Order of Preachers of the United States of America

iUniverse, Inc.

New York   Bloomington

Vocation in Black and White
Dominican Contemplative Nuns tell how God called them

iUniverse books may be ordered through booksellers or by contacting:

iUniverse
1663 Liberty Drive
Bloomington, IN 47403
www.iuniverse.com
1-800-Authors (1-800-288-4677)

Because of the dynamic nature of the Internet, any Web addresses or links contained in this
book may have changed since publication and may no longer be valid.

The views expressed in this work are solely those of the author and do not necessarily reflect
the views of the publisher, and the publisher hereby disclaims any responsibility for them.

ISBN: 978-0-595-47680-0 (pbk)
ISBN: 978-1-4401-2747-2 (cloth)
ISBN: 978-0-595-91944-4 (ebk)

Printed in the United States of America

Graphic design for cover: Sister Mary Catharine Perry, OP
Picture on cover: Eighteen Blessed of the Dominican Order, Nation Gallery, London (NG663:3-4). Used with permission.

Unless otherwise noted, quotations from scripture and the Church Fathers are taken from *The Liturgy of the Hour: according to the Roman Rite*, Catholic Book Publishing Co., New York, 1975.

In gratitude for 800 years of grace.

Contents

FRATRES ORDINIS PRÆDICATORUM
CURIA GENERALITIA

November 15, 2007
Feast of St. Albert the Great

Dear Sisters and all who read and ponder the meaning of these stories,

The 800th anniversary of the foundation of the Nuns of the Order of Preachers has been a great blessing for the whole Order, but in a unique way for each nun in every monastery. Throughout all of the Jubilee year of 2007, the monasteries throughout the world have held celebrations inviting their local Churches to give thanks and praise to God for the grace of being one portion of the "Holy Preaching of Jesus Christ"! Not only the local Church, but through the graciousness of Pope Benedict XVI, the Universal Church, in recognizing this grace, has made each Monastery a place of special pilgrimage granting the faithful the possibility of receiving a plenary indulgence. Indeed, our monasteries embody in each nun the receptivity of God's mercy and offer this same mercy to other branches of the Order and to all the Church.

It is with profound joy that I welcome this book initiated by the Association of Nuns of the Order of Preachers in the United States. It brings to an even deeper level the meaning of our Jubilee celebration. Ultimately, we speak about the mystery of a vocation, the story of a soul, the working of grace within the depths of each individual sister. For a monastery comes into being as individuals are called into community by the mysterious workings of the Holy Spirit. In this case, drawing them to God through the charism of St. Dominic. In reading the stories of the call of these sisters, one cannot help but reflect upon a theology of grace, which is nothing other than God's communication of Himself to us. Also, the incarnational dimension of our Catholic faith becomes readily apparent as this grace is mediated through so many people, situations and seemingly accidental encounters. Indeed, as the Acts of the Apostles states: "In Him we live and move and have our very being." (Acts 17:28 NIV)

Throughout my mandate as Master of the Order I have relied on the prayers, especially of our nuns, that the whole Order might better proclaim the Gospel of the Lord. And, through this time, I have been blessed to preach retreats, visit monasteries, and support our sisters of the contemplative life. This book gives me an opportunity to thank each sister personally for responding so generously to the call and invitation through the movement of the Holy Spirit in the life of each one. While only a few of the many nuns throughout the world have given a brief glimpse into their soul's story, we can more easily imagine the myriad others who have filled 800 years and, by God's mercy, will continue into the future. Thank you, dear Sisters, each and every one of you, for your holy vocation as living preachers of the Word of God.

Your brother and friend in St. Dominic,

fr. Carlos A. Azpiroz Costa OP
Master of the Order

Preface

This work came about through the collaboration of the U.S. Dominican monasteries and under the sponsorship of the Association of Dominican Nuns of the United States of America. Its hope is to aid those discerning a call to the monastic life, to recall the "first love" of those who have chosen it, and to raise awareness of Dominican contemplative life.

The following accounts are told by the nuns themselves. They are all true, although a few sisters prefer to remain anonymous. Given the many contributing factors and the mysterious element in every vocation, selection in what to tell is necessary. This choice was left to each nun. Any opinions expressed by the sisters are their own and do not reflect an official stance of the Association.

Acknowledgments

Grateful acknowledgment goes to the editors, Sister Maria of the Cross, O.P., and Sister Mary Rose of Joy, O.P.; to Sister Mary Catharine Perry, O.P., for all her advice and suggestions and for designing the cover; to the proofreaders, Sister Mary Jeremiah, O.P., Hannah Officer, and Nancy Carlin; and to all the nuns who shared their journeys along with the many people who helped them get it down on paper. Special thanks to the Very Reverend Carlos Azpiros Costa, O.P., for his introductory letter; and to Sister Suzanne Noffke, O.P., Reverend Michael Monshau, O.P., and Very Reverend Dominic Izzo, O.P., for their reviews of the book. In gratitude to our communities for providing the time and encouragement needed for the completion of this project.

Introduction

Dominican nuns? Few in the English speaking world are even aware that cloistered Dominicans exist. How strange for an Order famed for its scholars, teachers, and preachers! The surprise deepens at the discovery that this branch of the Order was the first to come into existence. In fact, it predated the Order's official founding by 10 years.

It all began in 1206. St. Dominic de Guzmán, a Spanish cathedral canon, stopped with his bishop, Diego, in Southern France on their way back from a diplomatic mission. Here they came into contact with a heresy prominent in the region, Cartharism: a dualistic religion that regarded the material world as evil. The Perfect of this sect received the *consolamentum*—baptism in the Holy Spirit by the laying on of hands. From that time on they were expected to live as dead to the material world. They practiced complete sexual continence, ate a vegetarian diet, abstained from taking oaths and bearing arms, wore a black habit, and would spend the day reciting the Our Father. The people, especially the nobility and tradesmen, impressed by the austerity of their lives, and many were won over to their teaching. Bishop Diego counseled the Cistercian papal legates sent to preach against the heresy, who up until then were experiencing little success, to adopt a more radical way of Gospel living to more effectively bear witness to the truth. To underscore his point, he and Dominic sent away their horses and retinue and set off to preach on foot.

Among the Catharist Perfect were widows, who set up houses with a few companions to educate young girls. Often these children received the habit of the Perfect, themselves, at the age of 6 or 7. The first Dominican nuns were noble girls whose parents, on account of poverty, had entrusted them to these women for their education. Converted by the preaching of Dominic, they still wished to dedicate their lives to God. He founded a monastery for them at St. Mary of Prouille where they would have a safe refuge, be able to educate girls themselves (a common practice of monasteries in those days), be a base for his itinerant preaching, and a center for reconciliation for people returning to the Church.

The nuns were originally officially under Bishop Diego's patronage, but with his death, Dominic assumed full responsibility for them. Dominic gave them the traditional monastic life animated with his own spirit. They kept many of the same practices they had followed as Perfect—a vegetarian diet, sexual continence—done now, however, for love of God and not distain for the material world. The nuns wore the habit of the Order, which was white—unbleached wool—not the black of the Perfect. When the friars came into existence, they attended to the nuns' spiritual needs. Dominic, himself, instructed them in the faith. At the time of the dispersal of the brethren throughout Europe in 1217, Dominic had all the nuns as well as the friars renew their vows in his hands—a medieval sign of fealty.

Dominic went on to found a monastery in Madrid where he sent his own brother, Mannis, to serve as chaplain. His only surviving letter addresses these nuns making it clear he intended them to live a fully cloistered and monastic life. At the pope's request, he also established a monastery in Rome to help reform nuns in that city. He planned to open a monastery in Bologna as well. His death prevented this; but it was carried out by his successor, Blessed Jordan of Saxony.

Today, there are approximately 4000 Dominicans nuns in 234 monasteries throughout the world on every continent except Australia. They live a monasticism marked by Dominican spirituality with its emphasis on the study of truth, the goodness of creation, and communal prayer and living. The prominence Dominicans give to the Incarnation is expressed through veneration of the Mother of God, especially through the rosary, and love of Jesus present in the Blessed Sacrament. The Order's goal is the salvation of souls. While the friars, sisters, and laity of the Order engage in preaching and teaching, according to their state of life, to further this goal, the nuns carry it out by contemplating the Word until He totally transforms them. Silently they bear witness that all preaching must be rooted in contemplation and consistent with one's life. Like the first nuns who kept Dominic's ministry in their prayer, intercessory prayer for the whole world's salvation plays a vital role in the nuns' life. As of old, they make vows directly to the Master General of the Order, and cherish their close bond with the friars. While not taking a vow of stability, normally Dominican nuns remain in the monastery they entered for the rest of their lives.

A few particular customs in the U.S. monasteries are worthy of note. Many monasteries here have adoration of the Blessed Sacrament throughout the day and, in some places, perpetually. The practice of the perpetual rosary, where there is always a nun saying the rosary, is another tradition kept by quite a few of the monasteries. It is also customary in many American Dominican monasteries to adopt some form of the name of Mary in one's religious name in honor of the Blessed Virgin.

So how does a person know she has a vocation to this way of life? There is no single vocational mold. Some have the desire from childhood, for others it comes as a complete surprise as an adult. Some are the pious type, others are not. Many have had previous contact with religious, but this is not always the case. Some actually originally feel an aversion towards the religious life. For many a retreat plays a pivotal role in their discernment, but not for all. Some have valuable guidance from spiritual directors, others never even heard of a spiritual director. Quite a few are converts like the first Dominican nuns, others are cradle Catholics. St. Thérèse of Lisieux seems to transcend the boundaries of her own Order, giving many a first inkling of the contemplative life.

Twenty-three accounts follow of how and when God called 23 individuals from diverse backgrounds, at different ages, and in different times.

This work deals with their initial call and discernment. Of course, that is only the beginning, but to describe the life of a cloistered Dominican nun, itself, exceeds the limits of this book.

Surprised by the Call

Sister Mary Thomas, O.P.
Farmington Hills, MI

If you had seen me riding down Davison Avenue in a 1956 Ford convertible, between my brother Tom and boyfriend Frank that Sunday afternoon, you would have thought I had it made. And perhaps I did. The two boys had come to pick me up from a weekend retreat at the old Mary Reparatrix Convent on Quincy Street in Detroit. A senior in high school, I had attended this retreat at the urging of one of my high school teachers, Miss Brady, who had noticed the Miraculous Medal dangling from the chain around my neck. This was in April 1957. I was to graduate in June and the retreat was for Catholic seniors who attended public schools in the archdiocese. "Why not?" I thought. If all went well, Frank and I would announce our engagement and plans for marriage the following year. A retreat would be a good time for me to reflect on that decision. I even asked the retreat master about these plans, and he approved what we had in mind.

Still, as I sat there between the two boys that fateful afternoon, I knew something was different. For some reason I found it hard to enter into their conversation. The new car, specially shined up for my homecoming, made no impression; and certainly neither of the two young men was interested in the fruits of my retreat!

In the days that followed I found myself thinking about the book I had begun to read while at Mary Reparatrix, *My Beloved*, the story of a Carmelite nun and how she entered the cloister. Try as I might, I couldn't shake off this preoccupation with "what, I knew not."

So one day after classes were over, I approached Miss Brady and told her that ever since making that retreat, I felt all mixed up about life and my life in particular. I'll never forget how she simply looked me straight in the eye and said, "Frances, did you ever think of becoming a nun?" It was the last thing in the world I had expected to hear. Silence. Then, "Well, when I was a little girl ..." Miss Brady reached into her desk drawer for a thick volume entitled *Religious*

Orders of Women in the United States. Handing it to me, she told me to take it home and browse through it. And oh, by the way, had I ever heard of the cloistered Dominican nuns on Oakland Avenue? She put a marker at their page.

In a bit of a daze, I put the book in my bag, left her office, and went home. Once in the privacy of my room, I perused the hundred or more pages of pictures and descriptions of every conceivable type of religious life and garb in the country, if not the world. The marker had fallen out by then, but every time I reopened the book it was to the entry displaying the life and charism of the cloistered Dominican nuns! And every time it happened I slammed it shut: *no!* They were too strict. To begin with, I didn't want to be a nun, let alone a cloistered one. That was the end of it. Period.

However, the discomfort continued, and I felt ill at ease every time I was with my boyfriend. I said nothing, but finally it got to be too much. I went back to Miss Brady's office. She didn't seem a bit surprised either to see me or to learn of my woes. Her almost immediate response was, "Why not go to see the Dominicans? *I'll* call and make an appointment for you." No ifs, ands, or buts. The matter was settled.

Well, you can imagine my high school sweetheart's chagrin when I asked him to drive me over to the monastery. And would he kindly wait in the car while I went in to see the mother prioress? Poor fellow, he didn't know what was happening any more than I did. At the time, I just wanted to settle this unrest once and for all and get on with my life.

Little did I know that God in His mysterious providence was drawing me closer and closer to Himself. Mother Mary Agnes, prioress, and Mother Mary of Jesus, novice mistress, looked at and through me as they peered through the double iron parlor grille that was standard for cloisters at that time. I answered all their questions with simplicity and directness, even telling them of the boyfriend waiting in the car. At which point I noted the reflex glances they made to each other, though they said nothing.

At the end of the interview Mother Mary Agnes asked if I would like to come back. To my own surprise I was eager to do so, my curiosity about the life having been amply aroused. When I answered yes, Mother asked if I might consider bringing my mother along. And here were some pamphlets I might like to take along to show her and my dad.

A week later I was back, this time with my dear mother who was having a hard time figuring out what was going on with me. We had come for rosary and Sunday benediction in the public chapel and would visit Mother Mary Agnes afterwards. I had not yet seen the chapel of perpetual adoration, but when I did my life was forever changed.

Mom and I went up the six or seven steps that led to the door, opened it, and were faced with the beautiful large monstrance enthroning the Blessed Sacrament in a niche high above the altar. It was flanked on either side by hanging chandeliers of lighted vigil lamps along white marble stairs that led up to the niche.

I was mesmerized, awestruck, and reverent. Instinctively, I fell to my knees and adored. At that moment, and in that action, I believe I surrendered my life to God, and by His grace and mercy, have never taken it back.

The rest is history. I entered the monastery in September; received the habit the following June; and, after completing my novitiate, made first profession of vows in 1959. Three years later, in November of 1962, I was privileged to make my profession of solemn vows.

Have I ever regretted it? Not for a moment. Have there been hard times? Of course there have, as there are in every life and every vocation. But our God is faithful, and it is He who leads us, sustains us, and continues to enthrall us all the days of our lives. To Him be honor and glory and praise forever and ever. Amen.

Late Have I Loved You

Sister Joseph Marie of the Child Jesus, O.P.
Menlo Park, CA

Late have I loved You
O Beauty ever ancient ever new
Late have I loved You
(St. Augustine, *Confessions*, 10, 27)

As I reflect upon the seeds of my vocation, I can only say that it was His hands that made me and shaped me by entrusting me to the loving embrace of my family, friends, and people I've met and by guiding me through the events of daily life.

I was born into a communist society but grew up drinking from the fountain of my mother's deep Catholic faith and wisdom. She, the saints, and especially the Holy Family were my role models. The Holy Souls became my dear friends through our nightly family prayers and rosary. My mother's persevering prayers, courage, and total abandonment to Divine Providence brought us out of Vietnam to the Midwest for the sole purpose of maintaining our faith. We were among the thousands of "boat people." Mom would often chant: "The devil sifts you like rice," and, "To gain the whole world and lose your soul, what benefit would that be?" These rich experiences and teachings made a deep impression on me and kept me thinking of eternity.

But really ... how on earth did I decide to become a nun? Well, the fact that I am now a nun is beyond my comprehension, for it is still a mystery and is completely the grace and will of God ... His plan since the moment I was being "knitted together in my mother's womb." While I was growing up, I never saw a religious sister nor had any revelation or concept of religious life. I was mesmerized by the wonderful world of science, but also always loved children and worked with them every summer during high school. I wanted to be a teacher, missionary, and mother ... my aspirations were endless.

Then came the reality and challenges of college life. It was then that the Spirit of God gently touched my heart. I was very inspired by the joyful presence of many young Vietnamese sisters and seminarians and the holy witness of Mother Teresa and our Holy Father John Paul II, who put so much trust, responsibility, and hope in us young people to build the future. All these ignited in me the flame of service to mankind. Thinking that this *insane* thought of religious life was just an escape, I pursued science. However, the Spirit kept increasing the flame's intensity as the attraction grew stronger each year. Immediately after graduation, I visited a Vietnamese community in California, and the sisters advised that I pay off my *huge* student loan first ... the debt that seemed to take a lifetime to pay. Upon returning home, I declined employment offers, with opportunities for graduate studies, research/teaching, then headed West to reunite with my sisters.

It was here in California that I truly met the many loves of my life, and the *One*. I got a good job and within a few years, jumped almost to the top of the ladder of success. God continually and patiently whispered in my ears, but the noise of daily life took over, and I was lost in the busy and restless world. I soon found every minute of my day filled with meetings, problem solving, socializing, more challenges, and of course, more meetings ... activities that seemed to crowd out the persistent and small calling of the Lord.

In the words of St. Paul, I boast only in the Lord for my success and the achievement of the "American Dream" in a relatively short time. He graciously gave me every good thing in life "overflowing and without measure," but I constantly felt a void that seemed like a great abyss. Nothing and no one was able to fill the emptiness. Daily Mass sustained me temporarily, and I knew I had to do something with my life ... *but what?*

I spotted a listing of the diocese's vocation office in the church's bulletin. I talked to the vocation directress, attended retreats and meetings given by different groups of sisters, and was quite shocked at the sight of sisters who were not wearing habits. Their ministries were meaningful, but somehow I was not satisfied and soon fell back into the trap of worldly allurements.

Like St. Augustine, God not only *called*, but then He "shouted, and broke through my deafness," and He "flashed, shone and dispelled my blindness." (*Confessions of St.* Augustine 10, 27) I often found myself in tears upon hearing any Gospel passages related to the *calling*, especially the story of the rich young man who refused to follow Jesus because he had much to give up. I began to have a deep spiritual thirst and yearning to know more about God and deepen my faith. I enjoyed reading spiritual books and praying and meditating during my quiet time in the early mornings. I started collecting and reading vocation stories, took the vocation quizzes, and knew beyond a doubt that the *calling* was very real. The Holy Spirit definitely melted the wax in my heart. Still confused I asked … *but where?*

Again God quickly sent lightning with a toll-free hot-line of the national vocation office in the church's bulletin. I called and obtained a list of various monasteries in California. It is true that as God closes one door, He opens another. I felt very attracted to the Dominicans. I was also thrilled that they had Internet and that I could communicate with them through email. A month of aspirancy within the enclosure with its merit and charm confirmed my desire, and I felt very content.

Throughout my confused and rather lengthy discernment journey, I always felt (and still do at times) discouraged at my own unworthiness, sinfulness, fear, weaknesses at not being able to let go of my loved ones and worldly attractions and the thought that some people felt called since childhood or never had any doubts about their calling. I often ran to Our Lady for help, and she gave me her Son as my personal spiritual director. He always reassured me through His Living Word that there is no greater love than to lay down one's life for one's friend; that I am His and He will allure me into the wilderness and speak tenderly to my heart; that I have not chosen Him, but it was He who has chosen me; that He will create a clean heart and put a steadfast spirit within me; that all things are vanity; that I need not be afraid but rely on His strength; that all He asks of me is to do good, to love justice, and to walk humbly with Him; and that He will give me a hundred-fold in return for leaving everything to follow Him and to risk my life with Him for the conversion of lost souls and of the world. Providentially, almost every time I came to visit the monastery, one of the sister's families would be here, and I would be invited for ice cream. Seeing how close-knit, and how warm, and genuinely human the nuns are, gave me much hope and courage.

On Sunday, October 13, the 85th anniversary of the Miracle of the Sun at Fatima, I decided to disappear into the sunset and imitate Jesus and His saints, who passed away from the world at the same age of 33, by entering Corpus Christi Monastery. I've been joyfully singing the *Magnificat* with the Virgin Mary each evening since and truly, "From this day all generations will called me blessed." (Lk 1:48)

The Dominican charism of following St. Dominic's quest for learning the truth and ministering to souls attracted me very much. I received the habit on May 1 during the beautiful Easter Season, also the Feast of St. Joseph the Worker, and recently made first profession of vows, also on May 1, amidst the

love and strong support of our Dominican family, my own family, friends, bene-
factors, the Church, and the whole heavenly court!

Overall, my heart is overwhelmed with joy, along with immense and endless
gratitude to God, as like Our Blessed Mother, I constantly ponder over the mar-
vels He has done for me. And *finally* the emptiness of my life is filled with His
Living Word and tender love. The full daily liturgical celebration with chanting
of the psalms and scriptural study quench my thirst. The silent time spent before
the Blessed Sacrament allows me to rest in God as He in me. I'm totally content
with my ambitions and desires to comfort Jesus because of neglects and abuses
shown Him by His own creatures, to embrace the needs of the Church and *each*
afflicted person of the whole world. All these are possible with just simple glances
at our omnipotent Eucharistic King, my Spouse and Savior. One of the many
great aspects of the enclosed life is that I can have personal, face-to-face encounters with our Creator throughout the day and a large amount of time spent in solitude with Him.

My friends ask what brings about all this happiness, and I can only describe
my joy through the famous words of St. Augustine: "You have created us for
Yourself, O God, and our heart is restless until it rests in You," and those of the
psalmist: "What can bring us happiness? many say. Let the light of Your face
shine on us, O Lord." (Ps 4:6)

For those who are still discerning their true vocation in life, I sincerely invite
you to come and spend some time in solitude … better to hear God's voice
speaking to your heart and to discover His will. Only then can you, "Taste and
see the goodness of the Lord." (Ps 34:8)

Sister Mary Mannis on her 85th birthday

Bea, the Baptist

Sister Mary Mannis, O.P.
(Known in secular life as Beatrice Lee Manis)
Newark, NJ—West Springfield, MA

I was born into an average Baptist family in the backwoods of Tennessee. I was the second of nine children. We had no running water, no electricity, no schools, no church, no stores, no anything! To get an education our daddy paid half of our teacher's salary and the county paid the other half. After I completed the eighth grade we moved to the small town of Oneida, Tennessee. Upon completion of high school I went to Washington, D.C., and secured a job with the government. At the end of World War II, I cashed in my war bonds and went to Kent State University in Ohio for one year. When my funds ran out, I returned to Washington and worked at American Chemical Society. Shortly after my return, I met Jim Wilson, who was the life of any party. Not infrequently we were the only couple left on the dance floor at the end of the night with the spotlight shining on us. Those were the days of the jitterbug.

A few weeks before he graduated from Georgetown University, Jim asked me to pray about us. The following week, when he picked me up, I sensed immediately there was something different about him.

We went to a party and walked out onto a terrace. We leaned on the railing looking in silence at the countless lights from the city below and the trillions of stars above as they merged into a single brilliant panorama. He put his arm around my shoulder and said: "Bea, I've decided to become a priest." I was speechless, dumb, silent. Finally, I said: "I don't understand, but I'm happy for you, Jim."

The next morning I called in sick and sat home for three days thinking, just thinking. "What does his religion have that mine doesn't? Never would I give up husband, children, and home for God." I called a friend and asked if she could introduce me to a priest, who could just answer some questions I had. "Make sure he understands that in no way would I ever become a Catholic!" I said.

That was the beginning of nine months of weekly instruction, though I did not realize that I was actually taking instruction. Finally, I realized that I believed even though I didn't want to believe. The day came, however, when I wrote my mother that I had "joined" the Catholic Church. In her response she said that she believed I'd be saved anyway, having been baptized as a Baptist.

I had only been a Catholic about six months when, making the Stations of the Cross at St. Matthew's Cathedral, without hearing any words, I knew beyond any doubt that the Lord was asking me to become a nun. I broke into tears and responded, "But my God, how can I? How can I, God?"

Still upset the next morning, I called Monsignor J. Arthur, who had given me instruction, and asked him what I should do about it. He said, "Calm down, Bea. You don't have to do anything about it. If this is from the Lord, He will let you know when and what to do." I was much relieved.

Sometime later I was a hostess at an Officer's club. An attractive young 2nd lieutenant came over, and I thought: "Is he going to ask me to dance?" He did! Not in his favor was that he was a Yankee, only about 5'11" tall, and I soon found out he was Protestant, too! Even so, there was something about him that really attracted me. It seemed to be mutual. We began dating rather regularly, and each time I was more attracted to him. The thing that attracted me most to him was the high regard he had for women. Like me, he had an inner need to share his thoughts and desires. Given that, our difference in faith was an obstacle, and this became more and more obvious as our relationship progressed.

One evening we were at our favorite place at Andrew's AFB, and the bartender said: "When are you two going to get married? You're obviously made for each other." When he left, Jonathan said, "Yes, we're laughing on the outside but crying on the inside." We again said, "Goodbye, this is it; it can't work." But it never was goodbye.

For instance, the following week I received a package and inside was a small beautiful red rose with a note that said: "Anniversaries are meant to be celebrated together … not apart. I'll pick you up at eight o'clock."

Time passed, and he was sent overseas to Korea. When he returned, he was stationed in Dayton, Ohio, so naturally, we saw very little of each other. However, on one of his visits to D.C., he told me that while in Korea he deliberately made acquaintance with a Catholic chaplain, hoping that with a greater understanding of the Catholic faith he might be able to believe. But all the answers to Jonathan's questions left him cold. He just could not believe. Truly faith is a gift. I did not want to believe; but I was given the gift. He wanted to believe, yet he did not receive the gift of the Catholic faith.

Another couple and I took Jonathan to the airport for his return to Dayton and as his plane flew into the horizon I stood there, watching it disappear. I knew in my heart that this was definitely the end. I felt as if I was experiencing a death.

Just before Thanksgiving, I called Monsignor Arthur and told him that I had to do something about my vocation. The time had come. He suggested that I see the Holy Cross Sisters, where he had previously been stationed. They definitely thought that I had a vocation and asked if I could enter in February. I said, "Oh, no! I could never be ready that soon." I left. My heart was breaking. How could I ever do this? The next day I called a friend. She suggested that I get in touch with the Dominicans. They gave me the names of five monasteries on the East Coast. I wrote and when the first two letters arrived I read them and set them aside. When the third one arrived, I read it and read it again. It had an effect on me as would a "love letter." So I promptly wrote to the Monastery of St. Dominic in Newark, New Jersey, and asked if I could come for a visit. While there, my heart was still breaking, and my one big question was, "How do you say yes to God?" That evening I walked all around the block, smoking a cigarette, tears streaming down my eyes, crying out loud. I wondered, "How can I, O Lord, how can I spend the rest of my life in one place with the same women?" No answer came. I went to bed so weary and thinking that I would never go to sleep. My head had scarcely hit the pillow, and I was out like a light. I woke up the next morning feeling as happy as a lark without any thought of the struggle that had been going on within me. When I walked into the reception area, Sister said, "Bea, you act like you're at home this morning." And I said, "Sister, I am," realizing at that moment that God Himself had enabled me to embrace His call.

I asked to see the prioress so that I might tell her of my desire to enter now. She called the Council. They questioned me and agreed that I might enter Christmas Day. On Sunday afternoon I called Monsignor and told him the news. He thought I should wait until after Christmas before entering since my family would always be reminded of my leaving them on this day. I agreed. So I wrote to the monastery and asked if I could change the date to New Year's Eve.

When I went to work Monday morning I immediately went to the personnel manager to tell him of my decision. He asked me not to tell anyone else until he had decided whom he would ask to replace me. But my joy must have shown because various co-workers asked if I had gotten engaged over the weekend. It pained me not to be able to tell them the cause of my joy.

I had only one month to get my affairs in order. I went home to Tennessee. On the train going home I wrote to Jonathan and told him that I would become a nun on New Year's Eve. I ended the letter by saying: "I will see you in heaven!"

My family was terribly upset. My father said that if he could, he would forbid me to go, although he knew he didn't have the power. My mother tried to delay me by calling the doctor to come by and see me because of a slight cold I had. She asked him to say that I was too ill to travel. The Baptist minister came by, and we had quite a confrontation with the whole family looking on. He tried to convince me of how wrong the Catholic Church was. Privately, each of my Baptist brothers and sisters said that they thought my answers were more forceful and better than his. Also, Jonathan called from New York, and we talked for a whole hour, laughing and crying. He ended by saying that he was happy for me but would have preferred my entering an active Order.

So with no regrets and a heart filled with joy, I walked through the Catholic monastery enclosure door in Newark, New Jersey at 6 p.m. on New Year's Eve 1955. With a heart overflowing with gratitude I gave myself forever to the Lord.

Forever Yes! Becoming a
Cloistered Apostle

Sister Mary Catharine Perry, O.P.
Summit, NJ

"I will never become a cloistered nun, never live in a city, and never live in New Jersey." These were my negative criteria during the time of vocation discernment. However, the Lord in His loving Providence had better ideas!

Ever since I was a little girl I wanted to be a nun, but in high school I struggled more than anyone realized with this question of religious life. It was always about belonging to Christ, being given over to Jesus. I wanted what He wanted—most of the time! Because the pull was so strong, I chose not to date. This sounds like I was a pious prude. I don't think I was. I liked being with my friends and having fun with them. In my senior year I decided that yes, God was calling me to religious life, and I looked into various religious congregations, but none really attracted me. Sometime that year I decided to enter the congregation which ran my school. I knew I wanted to teach, and I was also attracted to their semi-monastic charism. I entered three weeks after graduation.

While I remained in the community for two years, I was really unhappy but I didn't want to jump out at the first sign of struggles. Finally, my spiritual director made it clear that I needed to make a decision. I was about six months away from 1st Profession when I decided to leave the congregation. Making that decision to leave was the hardest thing I've ever done. I felt like I was jumping into a swimming pool that I knew didn't have any water!

Several months before leaving, the superior gave me the opportunity to go to Rome with four other sisters since a Benedictine we knew was being ordained by the Holy Father. I found I was bumping into Dominican friars everywhere! Even the monk's First Mass was celebrated at Santa Sabina, the headquarters of the Dominican Order. Afterward, my novice mistress, who had been taught by Dominican sisters and whose aunt was also Dominican, asked if we could see the places in the priory associated with St. Dominic and the Dominican saints. This

17

didn't mean too much to me, but during the tour I set eyes upon the huge framed parchment listing all the brothers who received the habit there from St. Dominic. I can't really explain this interior experience. It was very simple and quiet but affected me deeply. I "met" St. Dominic at this point: he became real to me and a father. Then a piece of stone from the ceiling of St. Pius V's chapel hit my shoulder and fell to the floor, and on our way out of the priory I slipped and fell down the main stair! So, I consider my Dominican vocation as beginning at Santa Sabina.

I knew that I had a vocation but I didn't know where. So I visited the Nashville Dominican Sisters; it was one of the happiest weeks of my life. I fell in love with the Dominican charism, and it was at Nashville that I knew I wanted to be a Dominican or nothing. I became very attracted to the Order's motto of *Veritas* and wanted that—or rather, Christ as First Truth—to pervade my whole life. I received my entrance papers, but every time I attempted to mail them I became very agitated and restless. Strangely, my spiritual director was not encouraging. When I told him that this community was everything he told me to look for, he responded, "I can't even get the classical station when I drive through Tennessee!" While there at St. Cecilia's I had the first hints of a contemplative vocation. The novices' schedule is very similar to mine now as a contemplative nun, but I realized it only lasts a year. I mentioned this to the novice mistress. She said, "Well, you should check out Summit." That went in one ear and out the other. Only *after* I received the habit here in the monastery did I remember that she had said this. So I wrote her and asked why she'd given me this advice. She replied that she didn't know: she had never met our community!

Every so often I would think about the contemplative life but would tell myself I wasn't the type. However, the contemplative life became more attractive, and the Lord was allowed to get in a few words. Yes, it was entirely possible that He was calling me to this life! I didn't dare say anything about my new-found attraction to contemplative life to my spiritual director because I was sure he'd discourage me.

Since the Dominican charism attracted me, I wrote to a few Dominican monasteries. An important thing for me was how the community celebrated the liturgy because my spirituality is very liturgical. No one, however, suggested the monastery in Summit, New Jersey. Only after I entered did I learn about our reputation for beautiful liturgy.

A friend gave me the monastery's vocation booklet. The photos weren't very clear, but the title struck me, "Do you wish to follow Christ?" Yes! He was the "heart" of my vocation, nothing and no one else! I wrote a short, cautious letter, and the novice mistress responded with a very personal one. One of her questions was: "Do you like to sing?" Do I!

At my first visit to the monastery the novice mistress invited me to make an aspirancy within the enclosure. At first I was hesitant but couldn't find any real reason *not* to pursue this, so I said yes.

During this time I struggled, wondering if I could adapt to what was for me a small enclosure, as I had grown up in the country surrounded by woods, fields, and a river. I knew God wanted me here, and that meant letting go of some things that I considered *essential*. While I didn't immediately fall in love with the monastery, I felt very comfortable and at home with the sisters. One night at supper dishes I left the kitchen and went down to the apple orchard. I kicked the ground, pulled grass, and cried, "No, no, no!" After that tantrum I was at peace: "Yes, yes, yes!" Then I got a letter from my director. For two years he had been praying that I would see I had a contemplative vocation!

One night during my aspirancy, I was startled out of sleep by the cry of a girl calling for help, then the sound of screeching tires. I knew it was something serious, but I didn't know what to do. I was trembling and shaking! This wasn't life in the country! So I did what I *could* do, I went to choir and prayed for this girl for whom I still pray. This experience brought a heightened awareness of the apostolic dimension of cloistered life.

Back home, I followed the sisters' schedule in my heart while at work. Finally, after a month I decided it was time to make the next move. Who to call first? What if I called my spiritual director and he said no. So I called the monastery first (after dialing three times and then hanging up) and *then* my spiritual director, who was much relieved. I then heartlessly bounced into my parents' bedroom and announced the "good" news. My parents were supportive but hesitant. Was this another temporary phase in their daughter's life?

I wanted to enter on January 6, the Epiphany, because it is a feast dear to me with its strong missionary overtones, but didn't dare ask. Well, that was the day my novice mistress suggested! It was a cold, damp day, and I came alone. At the last minute, while kneeling at the communion rail waiting for the enclosure door to open, I panicked and wanted to run down the aisle and out the door. Was I crazy thinking I was called to a cloistered vocation? I cried to the Lord, "Jesus, I am making a big mistake! You aren't serious about this, are You?" Once I crossed the enclosure door I *never* had a doubt that this is where God wants me! *Never*! I have struggled with my vocation and sometimes wanted to say no, but I knew I'd never be happy unless my life was a continual yes! My profession ring is engraved with "+forever yes+" as my way of reflecting my desire to live the mystery of the

Annunciation. It is in the monastery that I felt the desires of my heart and my apostolic vocation expand and become as wide as the world, while in the active apostolate I felt hemmed in and confined!

This is the bare outline of how I became a cloistered Dominican nun! There is so much more, so many struggles and failures, yet so many graces I received along the way. I am still just beginning, still learning how to love, how to surrender and let Jesus transform and transfigure my life into His!

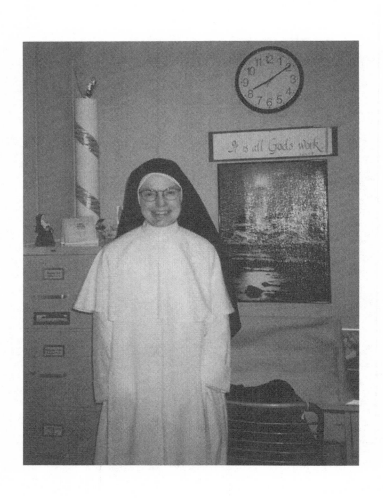

God Called Again

Sister Maria Cabrini, O.P.
Lufkin, Texas

My earliest remembrances of God were formed at Sunday school as a very young child. Presbyterianism was the faith of my parents, grandparents, aunts, and uncles, and so as an infant I was baptized, as they were, in our local Presbyterian Church. My brother, Bud, who was born thirteen months after me, was also baptized there. Together we attended Sunday school classes where we learned and acted out Bible stories. Those were happy times!

Shortly after Bud was born Dad had to leave to serve in active duty in World War II. About that same time our mother became very sick. Today her condition would be diagnosed as Postpartum Depression and could be treated, but back then, 65 years ago, this condition was unknown, and so she had to suffer it alone. She said she could have cared for one of us, but not both of us. However, because we were so close (Bud depended on me for everything, and I shared everything with him; we were almost like twins), she decided to leave us together when she asked Dad's parents to take care of us. This separation was very painful for us, especially when it seemed a long time till we saw her again.

When Dad returned from the war and found us seemingly abandoned by our mother and living with his parents, he filed for divorce and then put an ad in the local paper for a housekeeper to care for us, as his mother could not continue to do so (she would have had to put us in an orphanage if Dad had not come home when he did). Hermance, a young single mother, in need of a job to care for her baby, responded to the ad and, after several months, she and Dad married. "Mom" was a Catholic, so, after a year or so, she asked Dad if my brother and I could be baptized in the Catholic Church. Dad agreed, and after this we began attending Catholic school. This was our first experience with Dominican sisters. Dad took us to school on his way to work and picked us up after work, which gave us a chance to get to know the sisters better, and soon we became good friends.

In the 7th grade, Sister spoke about religious vocations, and it was then that I began to consider seriously the possibility of a religious vocation. I loved God and wanted to be near Him as much as possible.

Through high school and college I continued to keep in touch with the sisters, visiting them after school and asking them about their life. By my senior year of high school I felt sure this was what I wanted to be—a Springfield Dominican Sister. Up to this time my mind and heart were steeped in prayer seeking to know God's will for me. One day, while making a visit to our local Church to pray, I knelt at the communion railing and, after a few minutes, Our Lord seemed to speak to me (not to my ears but within my mind and heart). He asked: "Will you be My bride?" Immediately I said, "Yes, Jesus!" I was overjoyed and filled with peace.

During my next visit with the sisters, I shared this experience and asked about the possibility of applying for entrance. They were very helpful and gave me the address of their Motherhouse in Springfield, Illinois.

"Mom" was good to help me get ready, but she thought I "talked too much" and surely wouldn't be able to keep the silence. She gave me a year to stay.

Dad was concerned about what I was getting myself into. On his own, he stopped to talk with the sisters and, after about three hours of questions, he left feeling much better. I was his oldest child and only daughter, so it was hard to see me leave. He also worried that the way his marriage went might have discouraged me from marriage. I replied, "No, Dad." At the time I meant it. As the years have passed I can see that maybe it did have an influence on me. Nevertheless, God can use even difficult situations to draw us closer to Him.

Dad asked if I would wait for the June entrance date so that he could take me to Springfield during his vacation. As it turned out, he couldn't get his vacation at the time I needed to be there, so he put me on the train. During the interval of February to June I continued college, happy and grateful to be able to do something for Dad. Joyful expectations filled my heart as the Union Pacific took me to the convent. Two Dominican sisters from the Motherhouse met me at the train station and drove me to my new home. Eleven postulants awaited my arrival in the novitiate garden. All that "Mom" taught me at home really helped me jump in and live the life of the community.

Two years into my temporary vows, God called me again. This time, His call came in the form of a deep and strong desire to give myself to Him as completely as possible through prayer and sacrifice for souls in the cloistered Dominican life.

I was happy in my community and loved the children I taught, so this desire came as something of a surprise to me. Yet, it also gave me joy and peace. I prayed a lot about it because I wasn't sure if this were from God or me. One thing I did notice was that when troubles arose inside or outside of me, this desire was not strong. Only when there was peace in my heart did the desire come back and stay with me. This happened several times. I spoke with my confessor about it and he encouraged me to follow whatever God was asking.

It was time to speak with the Mother General regarding my desire to make final vows in the community. I told her about this "call" from God and she said: "Oh, that's seeing the grass greener in someone else's yard." She believed it was just a temptation to leave religious life. I believed her, and decided to make final vows in that community.

In January of 1964, my classmates and I made final vows and my heart was very happy at becoming a "bride of Christ".

Three years later the desire for the cloister came back. I knew then that I had to speak with our Mother General about it. We had a new superior and I would need to tell her everything, which I did. She was so kind and understanding. She said she was going to a meeting of religious superiors where she would meet the prioresses of our Dominican monasteries and asked if I would like her to inquire if they would accept a transfer sister. I said, "Oh, yes, please, Mother." She said she would inquire and then would call me when she returned.

Two or three months passed and Mother came to see me (I was teaching in one of our schools in the same town where our Motherhouse was located). During that visit Mother said that she spoke with three Dominican prioresses and all three said about the same thing: I should get a dispensation from my vows and start all over again in the monastery. I responded: "I don't think Our Lord wants me to get a dispensation from my vows. Isn't there a way that I can transfer to one of the monasteries?" She answered, "Yes, canon law provides for this, but these prioresses seem to be concerned that you would be joining them because you are unhappy with your vocation here." To which I said, "Mother, I believe Our Lord wants me here until there is a way to transfer to the monastic life ... If He really wants this, then I trust He will guide me. In the meantime, I will wait and try to be more faithful to my prayer life and to my vocation as a Dominican sister in this community." She said in turn, "If I were in your shoes I think I would say the same thing."

Years passed, and in December of 1970 God did provide through one of our Dominican Fathers who had come to give our annual retreat. As soon as I shared with him God's desire within me to transfer to a cloistered Dominican monastery, he said: "I was going to ask if you had ever considered the cloistered life." At that, I poured out my whole story. He told me about a monastery in Lufkin,

Texas, where he had given a workshop on Christology and asked if I would like him to inquire with the Mother Prioress if their community would consider a "transfer sister" from an active Dominican community. With my superior's permission I eventually wrote to the Mother Prioress asking if she would consider my transfer to her community. They invited me to come for a six-week visit inside the cloister in the summer of 1971. It was "love at first sight!" How did I know this was where God was calling me? I was not looking for the perfect community; I was looking for God, for His Will for me. I realize now that this "understanding" was His gift and with it came another gift—that peace which surpasses understanding that only the Holy Spirit can give. These were not things I could give to myself. Ultimately, of course, I knew that God would confirm this gift of the cloistered vocation through the community's discernment. That came to me in January of 1972 and my heart was full of joy and gratitude. At the time, I was committed to teaching until that summer, so I chose July 22 as my entrance date. As soon thereafter as I could, I spoke with our Mother General and asked if she would consider taking me to the monastery. This gesture would mean a lot to me. The news was bittersweet for her, yet she was very supportive and agreed to take me.

God alone gives the gift of a vocation, be it the married life, the single life, the religious life, or the clerical life. He also uses various people and circumstances to carry out His call. Many wonderful people have helped me to the religious life, both the active and now the contemplative (or cloistered); and for them all I am forever grateful.

For he who is mighty has done great things for me, and holy is His Name. (Lk. 1:49)

Guardian Angels

Sister Mary Joseph Kanja, O.P.
Farmington Hills, MI

I am an African and I was born into a Protestant family. All the family members born before me were baptized, but then came the war with the British for freedom and I was not baptized. I can remember sitting on my father's lap as he was reading the Bible to us children as he always did. And he explained how Baptism makes us children of God, who are meant to live with Him even after death. I was very afraid that I might die before Baptism. That lasted seven years; but then I was baptized. I was 9.

Attending the Protestant services I was left in need, always hungry for the Word of God. For this reason I kept asking, "Why can't they say all? They are not saying everything." I knew if they would say everything I would be satisfied. But I did not know what it was they were leaving out. The problem became unbearable when I noticed that when confessing the creed, we prayed: "I believe in the one, holy, catholic and apostolic Church." The words were a real puzzle to me. I asked my father to explain why we believed in one, holy, catholic and apostolic Church but were not Catholics. And what does the word "Protestant" mean? He told me that Catholics are under the pope, but Protestants are those who disagreed with the See of Peter. I told him, "But I remember you reading that Jesus said to Peter: 'You are Peter and upon this rock I will build my church.' Why then do we have to disagree with the pope, who is Peter of today?" I did not wait for his answer but I told my father right away: "I don't want to be a Protestant anymore." (This was terrible of me. Girls were not allowed to talk this way to their dad. But I loved my father so very much, that I overlooked, and so did he, some of our cultural restrictions. I felt I belonged to my father and I had a right to communicate with him.) My father agreed with what I said about Peter and the pope as Peter today; but he told me to wait until I was old enough to make a mature decision. So I had to wait; but I left the Protestant church at the age of 12 and for four years I was on my own, reading the Scriptures in the forest, for silence' sake.

I understood what I was reading as a love-letter from God to me. I came to the conclusion that I would leave home and go to live in a cave on Mt. Kenya, just with the Bible! But I was aware that I needed more information, which I thought would be found in the Catholic Church. One Sunday I was reading my Scriptures at a place not far from a Catholic church and I heard them saying, "Pray for us," over and over. I questioned myself, "Who are they asking to pray for them? Do I have anybody to ask to pray for me?" I continued to read from my Bible and the passage was from St. Luke, the first chapter. Believe it or not, the people in the Prayer House started to sing the *Magnificat*. I was really confused, because I knew Catholics weren't Scripture people. I was so moved that I went to the building's entrance to listen. At the end of it I had made my decision to become one of them. As they were leaving I made my way in to look for the leader. I found him and asked him how much I had to pay to belong! He just stared at me in amazement. Then he said slowly, "You don't have to pay anything. Give me your name and keep coming every day at 6:00 for instruction. After a year you will be baptized. And then you'll belong." Then it was my turn to be amazed—and I thought to myself, "It is all free!"

In a year I was baptized. It was a Saturday. On Sunday I made my first Confession and received my First Holy Communion. I had to walk 10 miles to the parish church and 10 miles back, but that is nothing for an African. I decided to let my companions go far ahead of me so that I could get in some moments of meditation and try to unwrap this gift package God had given to me of Himself. I felt the need to be alone for reflection. I was walking almost a mile behind and that was the moment I really meditated on my vocation. I wanted to give my all to Him, who had given all of Himself to me in the Blessed Sacrament. But I did not know how! I had never seen sisters or even heard of them.

I remembered my desire to go to Mt. Kenya and live in a cave. But if I went to live in a cave I would never be able to receive Holy Communion. So I thought about living with other girls who would want to live only for God, maybe with a priest to instruct us. Would the Church allow it? It would take time. But the desire was keen within me. So I decided to talk to the parish priest the very next Sunday. Was it possible for women to be like him—to live only for God. He explained—yes, and invited me to visit him when a sister would be there. I did not understand what a "sister" was. When I saw her she was an African in white like the priest, but with her head covered. I was confused and asked her, "Are you a woman priest?" She explained everything to me. There were convents in Africa for women, living together for God. It came back to me then, what the catechist had told us before Baptism about St. Dominic starting a house for women. At that time I didn't grasp what they would be and had forgotten it. The sister went on to tell me I could join her community, but I would have to wait two years. And I had to learn to sew.

God has sent "Guardian Angels" in many forms during my life. The most fascinating was when God sent a leopard! After my conversion, I was very busy in my family helping the young ones. Sometimes we would run out of water in the house, so, working 'til late, I used to take the path through the village in the dark to fetch it. I knew the path, but it was 11:00 p.m. or 12:00 midnight. There was no light, except moonlight. (I wanted to have everything ready for the children and not leave my mother with all the work. And so in the morning I could leave early to make the 10-mile walk to Mass.) The boys were very much after me, so I would walk along praying my Rosary. And every night—at the same time and the same place—I would meet a leopard! The path was very narrow. The leopard would move towards me on the same path with its two eyes slightly bent down, but shining red like burning torches. I would step aside (he never did) and he would pass. He was so big and so close! My back would be against the fence along the path. I would continue on my journey, but backwards, facing the leopard, who would turn and follow me. I used to have my hair fixed and tied up, but in the fear of this meeting my hair would always collapse. It was the same every night. I never got used to it.

When I reached the watering place, the leopard would wait for me at a distance of about 20 yards in a shaded place. And then, going back, he would lead the way. He would turn at intervals to see if I was following. When we reach my home, the faithful leopard would go beyond my gate and stop. I would enter the gate and he would come to stand at the gate and watch me enter the house. I knew he was protecting me, but it was a truly awesome experience—God sending a leopard every night! My life has been like that journey through the dark forest: alone, not seeing the end of the path. But God has provided for every step of the way.

After waiting for two years, I was confirmed. The sisters were starting a sewing school, which I joined and I learned all there was to be learned, to the point of becoming a teacher. But when the government inspector said he would give me a certificate only if I had an affair with him. I said, "No!" I left the room and told the sister I failed and what had happened. She said, "Fine," and we went back to the convent. I had already begun there. So I lived the life of that convent for three and a half years. Just before first profession of vows I felt I was not fully grounded to be sent to the missions and so I asked permission to leave. At the gate in tears I uttered a prayer: "Lord, you know my heart. You know why I entered and You know why I'm leaving. I need You more. Please let the saint of this day be my guardian and direct me to do Your will. But not now. I need five years to start anew."

So I left the sisters and I went home. Then I gave my address to my parish priest and asked him to call me if there was any available job in the parish. And he did. He sent me over a hundred miles away and I worked in a parish for five years. During those years my director asked me, "How long are you going to work in a parish? Where is your future?" He had a book with all the addresses of religious communities in Kenya. I told him if I would become a religious I did not desire an active community; but we had no contemplative communities in Kenya. He replied, "There are!" And he gave me the names of five. I thought I would like to be a Carmelite because I knew of St. Thérèse of Lisieux. And I knew St. Dominic. Then the priest reassured me that he would write to introduce me to two of them. I told Jesus to choose. Whoever would reply. In a week's time the Dominican monastery replied. The other never replied. So Jesus chose for me.

Three years later when I was a novice in the Dominican monastery in Karen, Nairobi, I opened my file on St. Dominic's feast and realized that when I had placed my journey under the protection of the saint whose feast day it was, that day was August 8th—St. Dominic's Day! I was amazed! I marveled at God's work in me. I realized that there is a plan. God weaves it. But we weave it, too. It's up to us to choose in which direction to go! May His Name be praised!

In Search of My Ideal

Sister Maura of the Holy Spirit, O.P.
Menlo Park, CA

Canadian by birth, I was the eldest of three children. I had an active childhood enjoying my studies at good Catholic schools. Every summer I enjoyed myself with my friends at our cottage on the lake with no responsibilities—just summer sports, reading, nature, and the social life of vacationing teenagers. The other months of the year found me working long and hard at my studies. At 12, I had decided I wanted to be a doctor, so at age 19 I was in the first year Meds at the University of Toronto. I did not proceed far down this path of science because the study of the arts, philosophy, and finally theology lured me into more satisfying fields.

At the challenge of my spiritual director I initiated on campus a "cell" of YCS (Young Christian Students), a then-secret organization of the apostolate. It flourished and these exciting relationships provided opportunities for maturing in a network of Christian friendships. Private prayer was always a significant element and soon Mass was on my daily schedule.

Religious life did seem attractive, but I saw it as a beautiful way of life for someone else, the pious type. I had the normal dreams and ideals of love, the perfect man, marriage, and a good-sized family. Since God had so far blessed me with all the good things of life I more or less took it for granted that with the same liberality He would provide me with the perfect match—but He didn't! I was spending much of my student life studying and socializing among the cream of the crop, but somehow my ideal never crossed my path.

By winter of my senior year, I was feeling absolutely desperate. Here I was, 21 and not yet engaged! Never had I suffered such a radical frustration. There was nothing I could do but pray to the very Lord of love who understood the beauty of my ideal and surely had implanted the same dream in one manly heart. I could not understand His delay—all my friends were getting engaged or married. In my visits to the Blessed Sacrament each night in the lovely college chapel, I begged and begged; but I noticed my earnest pleadings being transformed into,

"Not my will but Thine be done," and once I had surrendered, I found the Love of my life right before me—in the tabernacle.

After graduate school, I taught philosophy for two years. I knew from experience now that I could never have the mental freedom for contemplative prayer in an academic life of teaching, so I went monastery shopping. To me it was obvious that it would have to be Dominican: as St. Thomas Aquinas, the highlight of my studies, was Dominican and the motto of the Order is *Truth*. I thought that truth was the fundamental answer to all the needs of my world of 1948.

I must admit that "leaving all" proved to be quite a wrench but it was on a cloud of joy that I floated through the large enclosure door knowing that the life I was leaving was wonderful and filled with love, yet blindly and glowingly convinced that my real life was ahead. I have been delighted ever since.

Sister Mary of Jesus on her clothing day

"Follow Me"

Sister Mary of Jesus of the Presentation, O.P.
Los Angeles, CA

I came from a little barrio in the Philippines where there were no catechists. The priests came only once a year for our barrio fiesta. I first became interested in religious life at the age of 9 when my aunt took me to her hometown. There I saw a sister for the first time. Although I had no idea what a sister was all about, I felt she was close to God and immediately I was interested in becoming a nun.

I decided to work right after I finished 6th grade to help meet my family's needs, and did my first year of high school at night.

My desire to be a religious was reawakened when the lady for whom I was working brought me here to the United States. I asked her as a favor to allow me to go to church on Sundays, and she did. In fact, she gave me the privilege of going to church every day, although she was not a Catholic. I joined the Legion of Mary and the Third Order Carmelites.

Seeing a video of the life of St. Thérèse gave me courage and hope. I said, "If a 15-year-old child can make it, why can't I?" So I started searching.

As I said, what attracted me to religious life was God. I wanted to be close to God, to be with God. I was definitely attracted to the traditional cloistered contemplative life. Therefore, I searched for a community that wore the traditional habit as this had a special meaning for me. I had no idea that there were so many *kinds* of religious Orders and contemplative communities! I didn't even know Dominicans existed: I thought a nun was a nun and there were no differences among them.

I was glad to be able to visit a cloistered Carmelite community, but cried when I learned that the Carmelite life was not for me; therefore I thought I had no vocation to the contemplative life. But my Carmelite spiritual director told me, "Keep on knocking, for the Lord opens the door for those who knock." However, my mother was very opposed to my desires.

I was 40 when I started searching in earnest for my vocation. I had some doubts and worries since I was older, lacked sufficient education, had little religious background, was not a U.S. citizen, did not know much about my faith, and didn't even speak fluent English! But every time I saw a sister I was envious and kept on wishing to be a nun.

I finally entered the Monastery of the Angels, a cloistered Dominican monastery in Los Angeles, without my mother's knowledge. Later, when I had a chance to go to the Philippines, I visited my mother somewhat apprehensively wearing the postulant habit; but she no longer opposed me. In fact, by the grace of God, my mother returned to the faith along with my sister-in-law.

I had no idea that it was a call that I felt that long-ago day when I first saw a sister as a little girl. During that time I felt the desire without realizing God was calling me, since I had no idea how God calls and how God works in the soul. All that I remembered was the great desire to be a nun at the age of 9. However, all I could do during this time was hope, for I could not even imagine that someday I would become a nun. The obstacles seemed insurmountable. Now that I recall the past, gradually it is dawning on me that God did call me. I didn't even realize before that He has been with me. God was good to me by providing me with a good employer who understood and supported me. The Lord guided me and provided all that I needed in the midst of all my troubles and problems.

Saint Vincent Ferrer, I guess, was also involved in my vocation. Before I came to the United States, I kept on hearing in my dream a voice saying, "The end of the world! The end of the world! The end of the world!" (St. Vincent was a preacher of the end times.) I never knew that St. Vincent was a Dominican priest since I had never read any literature on him. He was the patron saint of our little barrio. I only learned that he was a Dominican priest after I entered the monastery. In my dream, I also saw Jesus dressed in white asking me if I knew how to pray. I said no. He asked me if I knew the Creed. I said no. He said, "Do you know the Our Father?" I said no. He also said, "Follow me." I don't know why I said no because I had been praying the rosary; probably it was because I often fall asleep during the rosary.

During my search, I didn't know what Dominican monastic life was all about. When I saw the brochure, it was the rosary that attracted me since that was my special prayer. I was also impressed with the midnight Office. Study appealed to me the most: I liked particularly that they had study, because I wanted to know God and to know my faith better. I was especially attracted to the solemn celebration of the liturgy. I saw on a tape the rites of the Dominican liturgy and I loved it. I liked Gregorian chant very much. It was after I entered the cloistered Dominicans that I discovered the beauty of the Dominican rite and Gregorian chant. It was very solemn and beautiful. I am hoping that someday the Dominican rite and Gregorian chant will be used again in the Holy Sacrifice of the Mass.

"Ubi Caius, Ibi Caia"

Sister Maria of the Cross, O.P.
Summit, NJ

Until I was 7 and a half, my firm intention was to take Hollywood by storm and give Margaret O'Brien a run for her money. That changed on a summer evening in 1944, not long after my mother had put my sister and me to bed. I still find it difficult to describe the experience. I saw nothing, heard nothing, and even to call it an interior visitation implies a certain lapse of time that was not there. It was instantaneous light and love: it was He. And then it was over. Instantly, my star-marked destiny as Margaret O'Brien's nemesis had winked out. All I wanted now was to marry Jesus. I turned over and fell peacefully asleep.

In the morning I stood at my dresser, picked up a pale French holy card of a pastel St. Thérèse, and made an instant connection. "I'm going to be a nun," I said to myself, "and I'm going to be a nun like *that*." I don't believe I really knew the nun was St. Thérèse, although I did know it was a cloistered nun—not like the sisters who taught at St. Angela Hall or the parish school. Once having found out what kind of nun this was, I spent a good part of the next 12 years tracking down Carmels near and far. Two were within subway rides of my own home in Brooklyn, one in my own borough and one in the Bronx. Though it was a bit of a trek, I could (and did) walk to the one on St. John's Place. By dint of constant harassment, I let both of those prioresses know that I intended to return at 17 to whichever house opened its doors first. I also hit on several which were further afield, just in case.

As far as the family went, the whole idea was a big laugh at first. My Sicilian father, a doctor, was a non-practicing Catholic who went to Mass now and again. After hearing my avowals for a while, he became annoyed and then angry. My mother was a non-observant Jew who, nonetheless, felt that we children should go to church fairly regularly (and indeed set the example and came along—I didn't know she was Jewish until many years later). She was first puzzled, then worried, and then sad. My much older brother's reactions were similar to those of my parents, while my sister was fine about the whole thing. However, when Dad

40

and Mother asked me why, I found it very difficult to come out with the simple reason I had for wanting to do this: that I was blindingly and irretrievably in love. So I fell back on the stubborn-sounding, "Because I want to."

Later on, to mollify them somewhat, I would point out that if I tried entering a convent while I was still really young and it didn't work out (although I had no doubts that it would), I could then go on to college or a career. This seemed to calm them down. My problem now was getting into one or another of the Carmels I had targeted. Without exception, the answer was that there was no room at that time. Each place, it seemed, had a waiting list half a yard long, and none of the more venerable nuns planned on dying anytime soon. And then, invariably, each prioress would suggest that I: 1) go to college, or 2) get a job, and 3) come back when I was 21. At 17 and a half, this was akin to suggesting that I return in my dotage. To say I was discouraged grossly understates the reality.

Mother and Dad sat me down and told me very firmly that they wished me to matriculate at some college. Whether or not I actually graduated was immaterial to them: they simply wanted me to take a breather from my obsession and experience a broader education. Accordingly, I enrolled in the music program at Marywood College in Scranton, Pennsylvania, and had a huge amount of fun shopping for a fall wardrobe and accessories for my room. I enjoyed college, was not homesick, and made good grades (although, like many young people, I lacked an efficient method of study—as I found out later on in the monastery). But all through the year I could not stop thinking of where I should really be, and *what* I should really be. As Father Horan the college chaplain put it, "Find your monastery, Marianne. Even *your* Guy isn't going to wait forever." On the day after commencement when we were loading up the car, I told the folks I didn't intend to return to college. Two formals, one silver-blue and one garnet, were still hanging in the closet in my room. We left them there.

Over the summer, I got on with my music, filled in for vacationing organists, swam, and continued to track down "my" monastery—or Carmel, as I continued to think. But as the days swirled into fall, it became clear that I would have to look elsewhere. So I branched out into Trappistines, Poor Clares, Benedictines, and a more modern (19th century) semi-cloistered community with a retreat house in Manhattan. My mother and I actually met their Mother General, whose oddness helped me to eliminate her group from my list. The Trappistines were also dropped when I found out that farm work—with actual animals thrown in—counted for a good chunk of their day. Not for a city kid, whose familiarity with fauna extended only to cats, dogs, squirrels, and the denizens of the two local zoos. In March of the following year, because of all the "get-a-job" messages,

I applied for a nurse's aide position (opening salary: $38 a week) at a small hospital in Prospect Heights. I hated the very thought of nursing, but figured the experience might come in handy if I were ever appointed helper to some monastic infirmarian.

As spring (and my now 19 years) wore on, I faced the devastating truth: none of my holy havens were going to relent and open their doors a minute sooner than stated in their ultimatums. By the end of May, mood indigo had descended; little did I know that dawn was just over the next hill. Two of my friends were going for a quiet weekend to a smallish old-fashioned house run by some Trinitarian sisters in rural New Jersey, and they prevailed upon me to come along. The place was charming, set high above a road that ran along a ridge overlooking ravines where graceful trees waved lacy green foliage. In one direction was the village of Stirling, in the other St. Joseph's Shrine, run by the Trinitarian Fathers. The whole ambience was calculated to soothe and calm one bruised Brooklyn spirit. I was finally able to give up and let go. "Okay, Darling," I said, "I surrender. You show me. I'll enter the first place that takes me without the job-college-wait rigmarole. That will be my sign it's where *You* want me, and then *we* can get on with it."

No sooner said than done. The evening before we were to go back to New York, Father George Huber at St. Joseph's, chatting with the three of us, told us that before we left we had to see "the Rosary Shrine in Summit," and that he would drive us over. In fact, he would do it right then. So we piled into his car and he drove several towns over, stopping at the entrance to a golden-stoned Gothic church set above a hilly sweep of lawn. On the steps was a nun. I gaped and turned to Father Huber.

"Is this a *monastery?*"

A bit taken aback, the priest answered, "Yes, they're cloistered Dominican nuns."

"It's a *cloister?*" I was beyond acting normal. This was incredible.

"Um, yes," said Father Huber. "Sort of like the Carmelites."

I'd never heard of cloistered Dominicans, and, of course, they were different from the Carmelites, but it was a start. We got out of the car. The nun was an extern sister who showed us the magnificent vaulted chapel, with the distant monstrance shimmering on its throne. "You sure work fast," I whispered. The sister asked if we would like to see Reverend Mother, and offered to ring for her. Mother Mary came to the parlor, opened the panels behind the black double grille, and introduced herself. She told us about the nuns and the house, we told her something about ourselves and where we were from. My mind was racing, though, and I was scarcely paying attention. When Mother asked if we had any questions, I said, "Yes: how do you get in here?" "You need an application form," she said smiling. My heart was right up there near my tonsils. "May I have one?" I said. "Of course, dear," she responded, and left to get it.

I floated back to the car. "I can't believe it," I kept saying, "I can't believe it …" Father Huber kept saying, "Well, what do you know!? What do you know …" At the house I phoned my mother: I couldn't possibly wait until I got home to tell her.

"Mom! I've found my monastery!" I blurted.

"You have?" she said, sounding a bit uncertain. "Where is it?"

"It's here in Jersey," I answered. "In Summit."

"Where is that?" she asked.

"I don't know," I said helpfully. "They're cloistered Dominicans." I knew what her next question would be, and it was.

"What do they wear?"

"Oh, Mom," I said, "it's a white habit and a black veil."

"White!" she exclaimed. "Mimi, you in a white dress? It'll be in the cleaner's every week!"

That was 49 years ago, and Mother was wrong: it's *never* been in the cleaner's.

The Church Is Catholic

Sister Maria Carmela of the Heart of Jesus, O.P.
Menlo Park, CA

I was born of Mexican parents, in Holtville, California, in the Imperial Valley. At the grand old age of 11 months, we moved to the San Joaquin Valley, where we settled in Planada, a small town with a population of 1,500, which is also on the way to Yosemite National Park on Highway 140.

Growing up in this farming town of mostly Mexican people, the church filled with them on Sundays, I just presumed that only Mexicans belonged to this Church. I remember as a child, seeing Anglos at church and wondering to myself, "What are they doing here?" I was amazed as I grew up, to discover that the Church was Catholic, that is, universal.

I remember being taken out of school to attend catechism classes taught by the Sisters of the Atonement. Later on, when we moved to Merced after high school graduation, I would go with Sister Carmelita to visit the camps where the migrant workers lived.

But, it was while I was still in Planada that I first received the call to the religious life, when I was about 16 or 17. I had no idea what religious life was all about, as after catechism classes as a child, I never again saw a sister. The only thing I knew was that they wore a habit and that only their faces could be seen. One day, I even tried using towels to see what I looked like with my hair all covered up. However, this phase passed and I continued to be more interested in boys and earning money.

Later on, after we moved to Merced, I again received another "calling." This time it frightened me as it was stronger and I didn't know what to make of it. I kept it a secret until I knew I had to do something about it. At this time, I only knew about the active religious life. Years later, I entered the Congregation of St. Catherine of Siena of Kenosha, Wisconsin, a Dominican congregation that ran Mercy Hospital in Merced, California, where I was working at the time.

It was in Peru as a missionary, that I actually received my first calling to the contemplative life. I went to talk with the prioress of a Dominican monastery in

Trujillo, about an hour from Casa Grande, a sugar plantation where I taught catechism.

The prioress was ready to receive me after just my first talk with her, but I thought better of it, as I couldn't just leave my country and family.

It was after I had returned to the States that I got my second calling to the contemplative life. I thought at first that the Lord wanted me to start a monastery and so I talked with the Bishop of Fresno. But, since I didn't have a group ready to begin this foundation, he told me to search further and see what it was the Lord was asking of me.

My search led me to work for the Diocese of San Jose and to make a retreat at El Retiro, a Jesuit retreat house. It was during this retreat that I was given more light and was advised by my retreat master to seek spiritual direction, which I did. I was directed by one of the Jesuit priests for a year.

And so, working at the Chancery for the Diocese of San Jose and with spiritual direction, I came to find the "road" that I was to follow which eventually lead to Corpus Christi Monastery in Menlo Park, California.

Of Toothpaste and Dominic

My vocation came before I had received the sacraments of initiation in the Catholic Church: it was a step in a conversion process that God had been trying to accomplish in me for some time. I was 19 and a student at an art and design college. Although I attended public school for most of my life and experienced the violence of an inner city atmosphere, I gradually felt in my heart a tremendous sense that this world is passing away, and that all things are nothing without God. As time passed, the polarization between the secular and the sacred laid bare such a contrast, that I wanted to do what I had read about in a second-hand church history book. I wanted to lead the life of the martyrs and the desert fathers who left the world, not because they could not live in it, but because they loved it so much that they wanted to sacrifice themselves in a most radical way for its greater good: salvation in Jesus Christ.

One day, as I was going into the bathroom to brush my teeth, I saw distinctly the image of St. Dominic in my mind and a feeling of assurance and happiness flowed into me. It was an answer to prayer. For a while I had been drawn to dedicate my life to God, but the many choices among religious Orders had thoroughly confused and bewildered me. After that moment, I felt this was it: the Dominicans—but I was still only half-convinced. Later that same day at Mass, however, a sister in a black-and-white habit walked down the aisle just as I was praying about my vocation. Then I knew that I had to raise the white flag of surrender.

My first step was to tell my confirmation sponsor about my desire to be a Dominican. He told me, though, that I was too young and that it would be best to wait; and he was right: I had not yet entered the Church and had just begun to live life on my own. But there was an inner pull that could not be quieted. One day I called my parents and told them, and they were quite shocked and opposed to this new venture. Graphic design was the beloved world of my father, and we'd had a unique closeness since I had decided to follow in his footsteps. But my parents were also open. It was this openness that led me to the Catholic Church in the first place, with their having taken me to a Catholic school for a time despite their Protestant beliefs.

One morning I awoke with the realization that continuing with school was useless, and I decided to quit in the middle of the trimester. I thought I might work for a while, but when I couldn't find work where I was living, I moved back home with my parents. There I wrote to our local archbishop thanking him for his stance on a particular issue. I hadn't really intended to ask about my vocation, but had mentioned it as a kind of sidebar. The return letter contained two addresses: the first to a congregation of Dominican teaching sisters, and the second to a cloistered monastery of Dominican nuns.

I wrote to the apostolic community and received several pamphlets which impressed me, so I flew off to explore the life of a teaching sister. I was attracted by their liturgical life and prayer in the chapel. However, I felt that there was something confining in the very specific apostolate of teaching—even though it could have been teaching art. I felt that my mission was to more than that—to the world, in fact. I sat in the sisters' phone booth looking down at the cloistered nuns' number and feeling more than a bit frightened. I could only imagine the hardships and the austere dreariness of their life; it seemed to me more like living in Auschwitz than praising God. I didn't think I could last, but something deep down said that I should at least try. After all, it would only be a little visit and I could still return home. The still more fearsome thought was imagining my parents' grief at my living a life of enclosure and separation from them and the world.

Later that year, I visited the nuns and found their life to be very beautiful—and much different from what I had imagined. I fell in love with the sisters and the monastic life, and yet there was something deep down inside that said no. I struggled very much with this, and it hurt a lot. I thought the "no" I was feeling was a no to the Dominican vocation, so I turned to Carmel. I had asked God that if I entered somewhere I would stay there, because I knew I would not have the courage to leave, and that it would also be painful for my family. I found a Carmel listed on EWTN's *Religious Life List* on the Internet, and visited for a week.

If the metaphor of oil and water not mixing can be applied to a vocation, it certainly applied here. During that week, I again felt the call to be a Dominican, but I didn't listen. The Carmelites had told me to wait a while in my discernment process; instead, I made a nine-hour drive with my mom to visit in the extern area of another Carmel on the list. There were many things that didn't feel right, and the nuns there probably knew it, too: when I asked if I could come for a short live-in visit, they refused. Rarely have I felt so much pain and the absolute hopelessness of a situation.

The last reasonable option that had any appeal to me at all was a semi-eremitic community, but it was not to be. The first day, whatever interest I had dried up, and I intended to remain only long enough to return home at the expected time. It was a very long week. However, through this experience of a newly-founded semi-cloistered Order, I was able to see that God wanted me in an ancient Order, with the strictest enclosure possible: papal enclosure. I left with the notion that such an ideal life was impossible; I felt that God had abandoned me with no further options. I hadn't yet realized that in slamming the door so hard, God was answering my prayer to be able to enter a community and stay.

When I was at the Dominican cloister, I had heard about one of their fellow houses. By now I was highly skeptical of any success, but I got the second monastery's address from their web page. Not long after that, I went for a visit. Although I still wasn't really sure, I wanted to see more; so I asked to return for a three-week aspirancy. After my visit I tried to leave for home, but ended up staying an extra day (my birthday!): there was a blizzard in the city where I was to make my connecting flight. This was an additional sign, I felt, that God wanted me here: I *couldn't* return home! I began to see that God was indeed calling me to be a Dominican, that the inspiration He gave me at the beginning was truly His will, and that the no I felt at the previous monastery was a "no" only to a particular monastery. I saw that God calls not only to a specific Order, but also to a specific monastery: each community, even with the same Rule and Constitutions, lives out its vocation in a different way, through its geographical location and the different people that make up that community.

I came back for the aspirancy a few months later, and the beauty of the Dominican monastic life took hold of my heart once again. That, the encouragement of the novice mistress, and a feeling of, "Yes, I could very well stay here," was what helped me in the end to say yes to what I believed God wanted, and to the peace I felt within—*especially to that peace.*

Though the months of searching were painful, I am ever grateful for the experience of other forms of religious life which has been educational, and also a support to me in times of trial. Shortly after my entrance as a postulant, my parents came to understand and embrace my vocation with enthusiasm, even though it was a sacrifice for them. And God has answered my deepest prayer: to remain here and make Solemn Vows.

An Extern Sister's Vocation Story

Sister Maria Christine, O.P.
Menlo Park, CA

The call to a religious vocation is both a story and a living study that harmoniously encapsulates the witness Dominic envisioned for the Order and a response to the evangelical councils of the Church. When Dominic sent forth the first friars to go into the world to pray, evangelize, preach the good news, and become living examples of God's everlasting love and care for all humanity, he engraved the heritage we follow today. The same vision of St. Dominic that formed the Order also molded the extern vocation, which is a combination of structured community living faithful to the Constitutions of the Nuns of the Order of Preachers with a limited participation in the activities of the world that sends us forth to be living and working testaments of God's call to a vowed life of poverty, chastity and obedience.

When I speak at vocational discernment programs or with young adults who feel they hear God's invitation to "come follow me," they often discover that listening to a personal vocation story helps to clarify their journey and remove the myriad of questions that confront them. But to write a vocation story is a literary challenge, because vocation stories are somewhat inexplicable and ethereal. No two souls are alike and no two stories are alike; but one fact I can state is that I too began by standing in those same shoes, bewildered and confused by the endless number of options available and asking many of the same questions. While God calls each of us in a special way, he never sends a clearly-written letter. Instead, He gives us free will and copious options. If we hear the "call of a vocation" we must take the initiative and begin the tedious and delicate process to discern the when, where, and how to respond appropriately.

As far back as I can recall, I always wanted to be a nun. Where did this come from? I will never know. My family was not religiously devout; Sunday Mass was an exception rather than a way of life. Perhaps it began when my parents brought me as an infant to church on the Feast of the Presentation to be baptized? Did God whisper the call of a vocation then? This is pure speculation, but I do know with absolute certainty that God in His own sense of divine providence placed me under His mother and grandmother's protective care, and that it began with the rosary. The rosary is powerful, and praying the mysteries nurtured my vocation. Then, there was the annual parish novena to good St. Anne. The entire neighborhood would save the 10 days of July to gather together on the hot summer nights to be spiritually nourished by the singing, preaching, and sacraments provided by the Redemptorist Fathers. I read every book on spirituality that was available, and gradually the embers of a vocation were strengthened and I was prepared to take up the journey. But where was I headed?

In the late '60s when religious life was in turmoil and communities were rapidly changing, and sometimes disappearing, I remained confident that God was calling me to religious life. The original call to a vocation was a childhood fantasy, a dream that made little sense. It was a vocation I knew little about, except for observing the presence of sisters in our parish and school, and watching with great interest some of the Hollywood classics like *The Bells of St. Mary's*, *The Nun's Story* and *The Sound of Music*. All of this touched my heart and stirred my spirit to search for the deeper truths of my faith. The presence of nuns profoundly influenced my life, and by high school I spent every summer as a volunteer "candy striper" working with the sisters at our local Catholic hospital, observing their life and seriously discerning my unceasing inner yearning. At one point, I was firmly convinced that God was calling me to a missionary life of nursing and caring for others.

But as Vatican II continued to impact the traditional religious lifestyle and big changes were looming in the horizon, I stepped back to wait and be open to the opportunities God placed before me. In retrospect, I now see how the next 10 years were filled with God's gift of time to nurture my faith, establish a career, and develop skills that would become valuable building blocks in His divine plan for me. God turned my life around 180 degrees. I discovered the Dominican Order, became a member of the Dominican Laity, studied apologetics and church history, was active in our local churches, volunteered for CCD programs, and socialized with many other young Catholic adults. Despite holding down a full-time and demanding position with a certified public accounting firm that frequently required long hours, especially during the income tax season, I was never distracted from God. However, the greatest mystery that unfolded was that I gradually came to recognize that my inner yearning for an active religious life was changing, and that the focus was now upon the contemplative life. I found myself very content when role playing and thinking about the possibility of remaining forever in one place. Yes, I wanted to offer the ultimate gift of perpetual prayer for those living and working in the missions and those physically and spiritually caring for the needs of all God's people.

I truly believe that with God nothing happens by accident. I was already attending Mass at the local Carmelite monastery, but the Dominican monastery, only 20 miles from home, had an irresistible power that kept drawing me back. The chapel of Perpetual Adoration felt like home and all the allurements of life in the world began to take second place. I found myself surrounded with new friends who were also discerning their vocations, and in this faithful companionship we visited all the communities we were collectively attracted to. We compared our observations and analyzed the differences and discussed why one was attracted to the Poor Clares or Carmelites, Missionaries of Charity or Daughters of Charity, Dominicans or Franciscans. In the process we prayed together and with the guidance of good spiritual directors each one of us soon discovered our personal vocation.

Filled with doubt and uncertainty, I could hardly believe that God really wanted me; but soon the hunger and thirst for a life of prayer overpowered my fears. My Dominican spiritual director told me about how Corpus Christi Monastery in Menlo Park had begun an "aspirancy program" for serious candidates and how it was designed as an introductory 30-day experience of living within the cloister—living the life. I knew this was my next step.

It wasn't easy to leave the security of the world I knew but these are some of the happiest moments of my vocation journey. After clearing the calendar and requesting 30 days of vacation, I "tried" my vocation. I was a night person, not a morning person, and the 5:00 a.m. bell that rang in the dormitory was jarring to my body and soul. A definite negative in my book! The days were long and structured, but after Night Prayers I literally fell into bed and wanted to keep reading every book in the library. Each hour during the night I could hear the rattle of rosaries as the nuns silently replaced each other and kept the nocturnal adoration. I thought: "Do they ever sleep?" In those days the community was nearly 50 strong, and personal space was at a premium. In the refectory we ate our meals in silence as a sister read to nourish our souls. The meals were plain, meatless, and often only warmish as we served ourselves on heavy drab brown plates and poured our drink into a round blue pottery bowl with double handles. Manual labor was plentiful and we helped to harvest and prepare all the fruits and vegetables the gardens produced and lent a helping hand wherever possible. We prayed hard, studied with enthusiasm, and worked with all our strength; but religious life is a *voluntary* poverty and all was offered to God with exuberant uplifted hands and hearts.

None of the allurements of the world could compete with or deter my resolution to return, to knock and seek, and follow God's invitation. The radical simplicity of the life was a treasure, and, on the feast of St. Vincent de Paul, my Dominican vocation crossed from the world to the monastery. The special vocation to be an "extern" sister, who would leave the cloister to further God's work, was an added calling that I could not resist. It is here that I could become God's instrument and be true to my vocation.

I have now celebrated my Silver Jubilee of profession and the years have changed many of the details I write about. The microwaves and steam table now provide hot meals, electronics have silenced the house from the annoying school bell that was once used to ring for a sister, and computers have replaced many of the old manual methods of correspondence, accounting, music reproduction, and art design. Most importantly, though, the essential elements remain, and with faith and the knowledge of God's ultimate love for us, the little sacrifices we make become our personal gifts of love, freely given for the glory of God. Nurtured with the Bread of Life and the power of daily Eucharist, the sacraments, prayer, adoration, work, study, and community living, we all strive to be living instruments in the hands of God—forever.

Sister Mary of the Sacred Heart with her catcher's mask

Making the Call

Sister Mary of the Sacred Heart Sawicki, O.P.
West Springfield, MA

In baseball and softball the catcher makes calls to the pitcher from behind the plate by means of hand signals. When these calls are carried out successfully by the pitcher it can make for a winning game.

During my high school years, basketball and softball were favorites of mine. I loved playing on the basketball court; I loved the people and I loved the competition. But playing behind the plate on the softball diamond as a catcher was my favorite. I liked to be in the action and the catcher was involved in every pitch in some way. I played first string catcher for the Ma Manning Cadalettes. Our competition took us to New York, Rhode Island, Connecticut, New Jersey, and cities in Massachusetts. Our team received trophies for winning the league, the State Championship and second in the Regionals. We also played a few exhibition games with the World Champion Raybestos Brakettes. Our ace pitcher was Joyce Bak, and she had a terrific fastball. Actually, she was so good that I never had to make any "calls" as a catcher. I just had to catch the thing and I did!

As a student I attended Cathedral High School and followed the college course curriculum. I was an average student and had a secret desire to give my life to God as a teaching Sister of St. Joseph. But then everything changed.

One morning when I awoke, there were two words invading my mind: "Contemplative vocation." In time, I would come to realize that they were "signals" of another sort. But on that morning I did not realize that it was a "call" from the heavenly "Catcher." I felt more like a pitcher "shaking off" that "call." Where were these thoughts coming from? Me, a contemplative? What I knew about contemplatives was that they were quiet and silent. I was far from that—more like a chatterbox behind the plate and elsewhere. How could I ever be silent? I was too active. I would never make it. It just didn't fit.

But try as I might those two words would not go away. At some point, I felt I needed time to think and pray about this. The answer appeared on the high school bulletin board outside the cafeteria. Another student had mentioned to me that there was a weekend retreat for juniors and seniors. Although some girls were interested, none came through. Either their mothers would not let them go or something else was an obstacle. I would have to go by myself. I called the retreat house and asked for directions. What bus would I take? Would I have to transfer, etc. The Daughters of the Heart of Mary ran the retreat center and the sister I spoke with told me that she would call me back. She did, and had also arranged for two senior girls to pick me up.

On Saturday, the first full day of retreat, the Blessed Sacrament was exposed for adoration. The retreat director gave us conferences but I needed time to think and pray. So, during free time I stayed in the chapel and prayed to know what God wanted of me. "Just let me know what you want, Lord, and give me the grace to do it and I will." But there was silence. No enlightenment (unbeknownst to me, He was teaching me to be quiet in His presence). I was getting a bit discouraged; but as I spent time in His Eucharistic Presence He was at work in my soul. At one point I said to Him: "You know, Lord, I think you really do want me to be a contemplative." It was the "clutch" moment and at that very instant I just knew in my heart that that was what He wanted me to do. Yes, the Divine Catcher had made the "call" and I finally got it!

The retreat director was Fr. Isaias Powers, C.P., and in an earlier conference he had told us that if we wanted to talk to him at any time about anything, (even just the weather) we could knock on his door. So after a short thanksgiving to the Lord for his answer to my prayer, I made my way to Father's door. I think the first words out of my mouth were: "Father, I think I have a contemplative vocation." He was speechless and was probably trying to analyze the situation. Maybe he was asking himself if this junior in high school was trying to pull his leg or something. As I recall his first words were: "Well, I wouldn't want to encourage you." After that my face probably showed what my heart was thinking; because I was thinking that I wasn't going to get any support here and why did I come. But he must have perceived that because his next sentence was: "Well, I don't want to discourage you either." The next thing I knew we were sitting and talking about vocations. He had suggested that I write to different Orders. I had recalled a monastery in the area and asked what the name of the Order was. He said "Dominicans." Ah, yes, now I remembered.

When I was in grammar school my Aunt Pat was living with us. One day she drove the two of us up to the monastery and wanted **me** to go to the door for a prayer card **she** had ordered. But I didn't want to go. Me? I was a little girl. It was very intimidating to think of going to the door of that big stone building, which I thought she called a monastery. But she wouldn't take no for an answer and so I went to the door. The sister was nice, but I was so glad to get out of there. It was so strange.

Yes, that was the monastery that was in my mind. I pondered aloud and said: "Oh, yes, Dominican." Father then mentioned that there was another Dominican monastery in Union City, New Jersey. The Passionist Fathers were close to the Dominican nuns there and he suggested that I also write to them.

When I left the retreat center on Sunday, my heart was as light as a feather. My prayer had been answered and I felt that I was on the right track. Back in school I made my way to Sister Richard Francis, S.S.J. We had a talk after school and I spoke about becoming a sister. We were on two different wave lengths and she delights in recounting that I had blurted out: "I'm not going to the Sisters of St. Joseph." When she understood where I was coming from, the two of us went to look in a book of different religious Orders. I wrote letters to various Orders as Father had suggested. At this point in my life I did not tell my mother what I was thinking about. I wanted to be sure before I said anything. So I deposited my letters in the mailbox. When this not-too-bright high school junior started getting mail given to her by her mother, she realized her mother might just be suspecting what she was up to.

The letters arrived one by one. Some were in active apostolates and I knew as soon as I looked at each brochure that it was not the one for me. When the one from Union City arrived it had a very nice booklet in it. I went into the kitchen and read it from cover to cover. When I finished reading it, I just knew that was the Order. I even pondered how I could ever get to New Jersey to visit the monastery. But as I mused on that idea, I received a letter from the monastery in West Springfield. The letter said that they did not have any brochures, that it was better to come for a visit and it specified the best hours. So one Sunday afternoon I took a bus and even had to get a bus transfer! I asked the bus driver if he knew where the Dominican nuns were and would he let me off at that stop. I kept looking anxiously out the window for something familiar and even asked him if he was sure that this bus went by the monastery. He must have been amused. He did let me off right across the street from the monastery on Riverdale Road. It was a long steep climb up the roadway to the monastery, but I wasn't even thinking about that.

On this first visit to the monastery I saw double grilles before me in the visiting parlor. There was also a big stainless steel cylinder thing in the room, which I eventually learned was what they called a "turn." That was the means of passing things from our side to theirs and *vice versa*. Mother Mary Agnes was the prioress at the time. She must have been a bit surprised on seeing me because when I first wrote I purposely did not tell my age (I was 15 and my 16th birthday was only a couple of months away). I figured that they probably would think that I was too young and not take me seriously. As I had expected, she told me to wait a year and that if I was still interested I should come for a second visit. As I left the monastery, I knew in my heart that this was the place and I was resolved to come back a year later.

Towards the end of the school year Sister Richard Francis had said that I should contact the monastery during the summer vacation. It was important to know if I was going to proceed in that direction because if I was not, I would have to start making plans for college. So during the summer I looked at the calendar and noticed that St. Dominic's feast was on a Sunday (at that time his feast was on August 4). So I thought that would be a good day. Little did I realize that it was a big feast for the sisters. But I was not ready to take "no" for an answer. So in my letter I planned it so that they would not have time to answer my letter and they could not call because our telephone was private and unlisted! Great plan! When I arrived at the monastery, I asked to see Reverend Mother. The extern sister asked me if I had an appointment. I thought for a moment (because I did and I didn't) and then answered that I did. She left and when she returned she said that Mother would see me but that I had made the appointment! I was a little embarrassed but happy that I was going to see her. During that visit, Mother Mary Agnes had a few other sisters come in to meet me. One was Mother Mary of the Immaculate Heart, who fired away one question after another. I kind of liked that because I didn't know exactly what to say to cloistered nuns. I also met Mother Mary John Dominic, who was the Mistress of Novices (she too, was a Cathedral High graduate) and Sister Mary of the Immaculate Conception, who was in the novitiate at the time. They all looked so happy, and I was happy as I departed, being that much closer to the goal.

During my senior year, I continued my studies as well as basketball and softball. The Lord was making all the "calls" along the way. My mother was open to my vocation and came with me on one of my visits to the monastery. My father was not pleased about my vocation. He was a WWII Vet and during my senior year returned to the VA Hospital. My mother was a rather frail woman, 5'2" in stature. I had two brothers, Al and Ray, younger than myself. None of us realized how sickly my mother was. My grandfather came from Florida late that summer and my mother ended up at the Westover AFB hospital. She was terminally ill. The date had been set for me to enter the monastery on September 8. My mother was not expected to live through the day. The sisters said that I could wait until after her death and funeral and also take some more time. The Great Catcher "called" her home to himself on September 9. The Lord arranged that my two brothers would go to live with an aunt and uncle in Western Pennsylvania. My mom's funeral was on September 11. The next day, September 12, everything had to be moved out of the house, which we rented, so we would not have to pay another month's rent. My Uncle Bob and others came to help with the moving and storage. Later in the day, a good friend, Marcia Souvigney, and her mother called to take me out to dinner. Mom Souvigney had made my postulant's dresses, and had done many other kindnesses. Afterwards the family gathered at my Uncle Bob's home and it was there that I donned my black postulant's dress. Late in the afternoon, after the nuns had sung Vespers, my family was there to bid me goodbye. Weary and tired at the day's end, I was at peace. The "call" came in the morning and now it was evening, a long journey.

Which Order?

Sister Mary of Christ, O.P.
Los Angeles, CA

I was raised as a Protestant and for many years I wanted to give my life to Christ. The issues that brought me into the Church brought me to the Order.

I first glimpsed the idea of holiness in the writing of T.S. Eliot. In high school I was much taken by the Christmas Day sermon in *Murder in the Cathedral*. I was a Protestant at that point and while I planned to remain that way, the world was getting bigger.

The study of history showed that things didn't fit into neat categories. There is room for texture and richness in the service of God. It matters that Benedictines, Jesuits, and Capuchins are all different. "To be deep in history is to cease to be Protestant." This was true for me as well.

Coming into the Church scared me silly. I had to undo at once a structure of understanding and being in which I had lived and in which I prayed until that decisive step. Coming into a religious Order was not as difficult. There were no thrills, but much desire and an inner restlessness until it would come to pass.

I had seriously considered marriage. I was somewhat ambivalent and did not trust my reactions. While I did not put things off, I still remained something of a mystery to myself.

What I read about religious life was almost exclusively Benedictine, so I thought that would be the Order for me. I visited a Benedictine monastery and decided that it would *not* be the place for me.

I knew little about St. Dominic, but attended services at the Dominican House of Studies in Oakland. The architecture enchanted me. The ceiling contained innumerable shields of the Provinces, the flooring in black and white tile, lines of brethren in choir stalls worshipping God. Obviously, there was another deep, rich, historical Order to be considered.

Fr. Brian Mullady, O.P., whom I had known when he studied at Univeristy of California Santa Barbara, made me promise to visit the Monastery of the Angels if the Benedictine monastery was not right for me.

Although I had promised, I did not want to go from Order to Order looking for "the right one." In my godmother's religious bookstore I researched all the different Orders that might be a possibility. One thing for sure: it had to be contemplative. I was so frustrated that I asked Our Lord what would have to happen for me to find the right place. Did someone have to put their finger in a book and point it out?

Shortly after this, a fisherman, who was clearly leading a devout life and buying excellent religious books, came into the shop. He said a woman who was a friend of his wanted to find a place she could go on retreat. I opened the Diocesan Directory and found the Monastery of the Angels. Well, that may or may not have been a direct answer to prayer, but I did remember my promise and immediately wrote to the prioress at the monastery. I was finishing my degree at Berkeley and would not be free until I had finished another quarter and paid off my debts. Education in the campuses of University of California was practically free and I was not much in debt.

At the monastery I was deeply moved by the Perpetual Adoration and by the Divine Office. I felt sure that this was the place Our Lord meant me to be.

First Love

I don't recall when I first wanted to become a nun; I can't remember a time before I wanted to be one. Growing up near a Dominican monastery, we kids used to peep through the knotholes of the wooden enclosure fence in the hopes of seeing a figure dressed in white. There was no doubt about it: that was what I would be. No grown-ups looked happier and what better life was there than to live with God? Although we knew the nuns well, I didn't really have a clear idea of monastic life as a child. I simply knew that nuns spent their day in prayer. As I grew older, I was a little relieved to learn that they didn't pray *all* day long. I thought my knees might get tired. They cooked and cleaned and worked, too. Even better. So, my mind was made up. I'd enter on my 18th birthday, and that was that.

By the time I was 13, I began having second thoughts. My baby twin sisters were born around this time, which awakened all my own maternal longings. Guys were also becoming increasingly interesting, and the vow of chastity started to daunt me. I began to develop the attitude, "Well, I'll go to college and if I don't meet anyone I want to marry, then I'll be a nun."

At 15, while watching a nun make the prostration after solemn vows, a doubt as to the supernatural character of her call flitted through my mind: "Perhaps she couldn't find anyone to marry and that's why she's here." Then Jesus spoke to my heart, "I chose her, she didn't choose me. I am the one to choose. You don't decide to become a nun like you would a career. I love you and want to make you happy. I would never ask you to live a life that would make you unhappy. Do you think I would want you to be a nun simply because you had nothing better to do?" I was abashed. I'd been throwing myself at God. O.K., He wanted to make me happy and I wanted to get married, so being a nun was out of the question. That was settled.

Freshman year of college, I promptly fell in love. It was like being struck by lightning. The world turned golden. I spent three years in la-la land thinking about the guy. We were of different faiths so I never seriously thought of marrying him; but my liking for him seemed to paralyze any decision-making about the future. One of my teachers asked me if I had ever considered the single lay state as a vocation. I hadn't. Being 17 and in love, it didn't appeal to me at all. The thought of living alone horrified me. I struggled to be open to this option with scant success.

During this time, I read the *Confessions of St. Augustine*. The discourse of Lady Continence stood out. Up until then, I assumed people just gritted their teeth and bore the vow of chastity. Now I realized that it was a gift from God. Only His grace made it possible. If someone were called to it, God would be at his or her side to help. I couldn't help thinking, "If Augustine could do it, *anyone* could."

Christmas break of senior year, I finally realized that I was rather idealizing the guy I liked, which effectively cured me of the infatuation. After graduation, I had to face the fact that, like it or not, I was a single lay woman. I decided I'd like to teach at the college level, philosophy being my main interest. I took a job half way across the country from my hometown as a bookkeeper and librarian at the school I had attended, with plans of paying off my loans as quickly as possible and then going on for my Master's. I lived with two other girls and found that the single life wasn't so bad. However, there was a sense of emptiness. We were pretty much three individuals living together. There wasn't that mutual interdependence as in family life. Life seemed stale, flat. Through a series of unexpected events I did end up teaching a college class. Although I loved the students and teaching, I quickly realized it wasn't really something to which I could devote my whole life. I wanted a job that was 24/7. I wanted to give my life to someone.

That fall, I attended a talk by a Benedictine monk about his recent trip to China. One slide showed a Buddhist nun. He told of how she endured years of persecution from the Communist government. Now that things were relaxing, other young women were joining her. *Interior earthquake*: my whole world turned upside down. I rushed out of the auditorium with her picture clearly in my mind. Here she was, a Buddhist, with no belief in a personal God, making great sacrifices to spend her life in fasting and prayer and I, who had the Triune God dwelling within me, what was I doing? Wheeling around on God, I said, "And You, it's all your fault because You haven't asked me!" That felt good. Such an explosion should have given me a clue that something was brewing beneath the surface, but it didn't. I could yell at Him all I wanted, but God was God: unchangeable. He had said no five years before so it was unalterable. It didn't occur to me that it might not be He that needed changing.

Meanwhile, I had gotten to be good friends with a man whom I was hoping would ask me out. However, when I sensed he wanted to take the relationship to another level, I felt annoyed. My reaction mystified me. Didn't I just want him to ask me out? Mulling the problem over during the Offertory at Mass, a wave of intense longing for the cloister swept over me, like what I had experienced as a child, knowing I belonged in there. I couldn't believe it. It had been years since I had felt like this. As I took the mail down to the post office after Mass, I wept from sheer bewilderment. "God, what are you doing to me?" Even with my long exposure to nuns, I didn't have a clue what a person did if she thought she might have a vocation. So, I didn't do anything and simply put the experience to one side. But there was a feeling of expectancy. Something was going to happen.

Two weeks later, eating lunch with one of my former professors and mentor, I mentioned that I thought this man liked me. "Oh, I don't think so," he replied (he knew perfectly well that he did and that I liked him back). "Besides," he added, "he might have a vocation." This was the last straw: *volcanic eruption*. Getting up from the table, I fumed interiorly, "*He* might have a vocation. *I'm* the one with the vocation!" The cauldron boiled for the rest of the day. After work, I stopped by two of my classmates' apartment. We got to talking and I was telling them of the different conclusions I had reached during the summer: I wanted to live in community; I felt that some sort of obedience was the only way to draw me out of myself. One of my friends is the sort of person to whom the answer for everything is "love." So for each point I mentioned, she replied that I should get married, to which I off-handedly responded,

"Or enter a convent."

"Well, do you want to start dating?"

"No." (I didn't really have anything against dating *per se*, but when she said, "dating," I was thinking "marriage.")

Stunned by my words, I climbed into my car to make the 30-minute commute home. Before this, I had had a feeling I wouldn't marry, but was rather annoyed by the fact. Why couldn't I just be normal? Now I realized that I wouldn't marry, not because I hadn't met the right person, but because I didn't want to marry. And I didn't want to marry because I wanted to do something else; or rather I wanted Someone else and always had.

The presence of Jesus palpably filled that white '93 Ford Escort, *LX*. I hesitate to describe the experience for fear of making it sound more or less than it was. It was like being in a room with someone you love but cannot see; yet, you can feel his eyes on you. He didn't say anything. He just looked at me. My own lips had just confessed that I neither wished to be married or single. So where exactly did that leave us? All the doors in my life seemed to simultaneously slam shut. Only one remained ajar opening to the monastery. And His look: it was like when a guy looks at you, not with lust, but with a desire that you be his girl. I knew God loved us and that nuns are called "brides of Christ," but I had always taken the latter term as purely poetic. It's astounding to have God look at you like that; both exhilarating and humbling because you know it's totally unmerited. To my surprise, I felt very much like when I had first fallen love, except it was magnified a hundred times.

A very direct dialogue ensued.

I kept saying, "What do you want? What do you want?"

The gist of His reply was, "You can do whatever you please. You can get married; you can have the job of your choice; but it would please me if you would have me."

I melted.

He had asked a question and waited for an answer. He wouldn't force me. It was powerful, but gentle persuasion. Never have I felt so free yet, at the same time, it seemed impossible that I should say no. I pulled into the parking lot and sat in my car, finally saying, "Whatever. Whatever you want, Lord." Then the presence that had surrounded me seemed to pierce through me and close around my heart. I could barely move. What did that mean?

I stumbled up the stairs to my apartment. One of my roommates turned and stared at me. I must have looked pretty shook up.

"What happened to you?" she asked.

"I don't know. I don't know what's happening to me."

"You're going to become a nun, aren't you?"

"Yes."

It was then that I knew.

A Retreat to Remember

Sister Mary of St. Joseph, O.P.
Menlo Park, CA

As I ponder over the past, I can see the grace of our Beloved God slowly forming my religious vocation. My first remembrance was when I was quite young receiving from my Auntie Celeste the *Little Flower Prayer Book*, which I loved to read. Besides the prayer, I am sure the book described St. Thérèse's life in the cloister and her early death. This perhaps was my first insight into religious life.

Raised on a small farm near Chico, California, I had a happy and very busy childhood. I remember attending Mass in Chico's Catholic Church, Orlands's Catholic Church and Hamilton City's small church.

After a postgraduate course from Hamilton High, I attended and graduated from Heald's Business College in Sacramento and worked as a steno-clerk at MacClellan Air Force Base. All this time, I was very faithful in attending Mass at the Cathedral of the Blessed Sacrament in Sacramento with my sister Neomi, who joined me when I started working. I can see how our Beloved Lord provided me with Catholic people as friends, even a Catholic roommate. I worked for a Catholic family when I attended college and Mr. and Mrs. Haggerty would take me to Mass every Sunday. It was a Catholic roommate who would eventually take me to the Carmelite monastery and introduce me to the nuns.

One day, the Cathedral of the Blessed Sacrament invited people to attend a retreat to be held there. The sign read, "You might be pleasing to yourself but are you pleasing to God?" I thought, "I better find out." So I asked a friend to go with me to attend the retreat. But that wasn't all: we were to attend an early Mass in the morning to reap the benefits from the retreat, and my friend didn't feel she could rise that early. In those days, Sacramento was a crime city, but I was determined to attend Mass even if I had to go alone. So I walked to the Cathedral in the early hours by myself, praying the rosary all the way.

Both the retreat and the grace of the Mass changed my life—I was flying high and the grace of God took over my life. I knew then I wanted to give myself to God. What I read in *St. Thérèse's Prayer Book* came back to me, and I visited the

Carmelite monastery on Stockton Boulevard in Sacramento. They were still living in the home that was converted into a monastery, with a high fence around their property. I became acquainted with the nuns and joined the Guild. The Carmelite way of spirituality, which I learned as a young Third Order member, made me long for the contemplative life, but the Carmelite monasteries that I knew did not attract me.

Once, my friends and I told Father that there weren't many Catholic doings in Sacramento. Father told us there would be a three-day retreat for Holy Week in San Rafael and asked if we would like to attend. One of my friends and I jumped at the invitation, and that was where we found out about the Dominican cloistered nuns in Menlo Park. We both loved it. I was never comfortable with the Carmelite life and here at Menlo Park, the nuns were so happy and their Divine Office was just beautiful to listen to (Gregorian Chant). The monastery was huge, spacious with 11 acres, and housed 48 nuns who led a very cloistered life. The inside cloistered chapel had beautiful stalls on both sides just like the cloisters in Europe, with the Blessed Sacrament exposed in a monstrance in the wall which separated the two chapels. Exposition of the Blessed Sacrament was held 24 hours a day with nuns in adoration. Who could ask for more? It was just like living in heaven on earth. There was early Mass every day and the public could listen to the Divine Office sung or recited and visit the Blessed Sacrament. After the chanting of Vespers, there was Benediction of the Blessed Sacrament.

I had no idea of joining the religious life until that retreat in the Cathedral of the Blessed Sacrament. It was the instrument of spiritual renewal for me. I can see how God was drawing me all the time to this blessed life by always providing Catholic people for my friends.

I remained active in Church activities and helped with the Cathedral library and religious goods store until I left for the monastery in Menlo Park. When I visited this monastery, I was delighted to find that I was born on the very day that the founding sisters had left the New York monastery to bring Dominican contemplative life to California. I was impressed with the joy that the life brought to its members who formed one big happy family. The perpetual adoration of the Blessed Sacrament and the singing of the Divine Office were aspects of the life that attracted me. Since I had found what I was looking for I asked to be accepted as a postulant.

Intercessory prayer is my special charism and my heart encloses the needs of the entire world and purgatory as I adore Our Eucharistic Lord each day.

It is He Who Leads Us, He is Our Guide

✦

(Ps 48:14)

Sister Mary Agnes Baudo, O.P.
Buffalo, NY

Having reached the golden years of religious life, I look back and see how mysteriously God's love has led me on the multiple paths of life.

Before He formed me in my mother's womb He chose me to be a Dominican nun, but He kept that secret from me until I was a teenager. The years I attended public grammar school were filled with the ordinary joys of youth; special friendships, baseball, roller skating, biking, etc. But the thought of a religious vocation never entered my mind during that period of my life.

My parents wanted to give me a good high school education so I chose a Catholic school. It was during those years that I was attracted to the religious life, and was willing to go to whichever religious Order God had chosen for me. I searched through a vocation brochure and began writing to several addresses throughout our country to inquire about the lifestyle of different communities. When the answers came, none of them appealed to me. After reading the autobiography of St. Thérèse, *The Story of a Soul*, I desired to dedicate my life to praying for priests. But I was not sure where God was leading me. My prayers for His guidance intensified. During my high school days, love for Jesus in the Blessed Sacrament grew within me. When I began working in a business office, I used most of my daily lunch hour to walk to the nearest Catholic church, make a quick visit to the Blessed Sacrament, then return to work. Those visits satisfied my desire to be close to the Divine Presence.

As I continued to pray for guidance regarding my vocation, there seemed to be only one of two choices: either Carmel because I felt drawn to the cloistered life, or the Franciscans in Williamsville, New York, because that Congregation had perpetual adoration of the Blessed Sacrament. I was not aware that the Dominican Order existed, nor that there was a monastery of cloistered Dominican nuns in my hometown. Divine providence arranged, through one of my friends, to acquaint me with someone who was planning to enter the Dominican monastery on Doat Street. When she told me the nuns were cloistered and had perpetual adoration of the Blessed Sacrament, I wondered if this was the answer to my prayers.

> *The Lord, your God, is bringing you into a good country,*
> *a land with streams of water, a land of wheat and barley,*
> *a land where you will lack nothing*
> (Dt 8:7)

I met the prioress, and, later, on September 12, 1952, after many visits, I responded to Our Lord's invitation to follow Him into *a good country* where He planned to let me drink from many *streams of water* and to eat enriched *wheat and barley*.

However, there was a high price to be paid before arriving at this destination. I cannot forget Mom's tears when I left the homestead, and I understood Dad's silence as he accompanied me to the monastery. Our hearts ached at the thought of separation, but at that time we did not realize what St. John Chrysostom stated about Christ's Mystical Body:

> Where I am, there you are, too, and where you are, I am. For we are a single body, and the body cannot be separated from the head, nor the head from the body. Distance separates us, but love unites us, and death itself cannot divide us. For though my body die, my soul will live and be mindful of my people.
> (St. John Chrysostom, *Ante exsilium*, nn. 1-3: PG 427*-430)

Indeed, the bond of love for my relatives and friends has become stronger since my entrance into religious life. Instead of feeling separated from them, love more strongly binds them to me.

I arrived at the monastery in the early afternoon on that memorable September 12. The sun shining through the windows caused me to feel as though I were in a heavenly atmosphere. The nuns led me in a procession to the choir where the prioress asked Our Blessed Mother to guide me through my religious life and to bless my loved ones.

I did not know what to expect of this new way of life in general except that I had come to a place of silence that facilitates a life of prayer. As the years rolled by, the Good Shepherd led me to *streams of water* which flowed through the sacred scriptures, the sacraments, observance of the Dominican Nuns' Constitutions, spiritual reading and doctrinal study. He provided *wheat and barley* through priestly ministry to sustain me through temptations and trials. I was nourished by the guidance and good example of the sisters with whom I have lived, and blessed by the experience of many duties which gave me opportunities to work with my sisters in the monastery and recognize their virtues and dedication to our type of life. Blessed be God for His goodness.

Lord, it is good for me to be here!
The Lord led me

> *Into a good country,*
> *A land with streams of water,*
> *A land of wheat and barley.*

Here I am in a land where nothing is lacking to me because *God is all in all.*

"You Have not Chosen Me, but I Have Chosen You"

✦

(Jn 15:16)

Sister Mary Thomas, O.P.
Lufkin, TX

Our Lord says, "You have not chosen Me, but I have chosen you." (Jn 15:16) This could be the theme song of my life. On the surface, there was certainly no reason to choose me! And yet God had His eye on me from the very beginning. Even before I was born, He was planning for me to become a Dominican nun.

I was born in Corpus Christi, Texas, my parents' first child and only daughter. I was born in a Catholic hospital, and I have often wondered if one of the sister-nurses might have baptized me secretly. This is because when the head nurse presented me to my father, he gasped and exclaimed,

"That's not a baby, it's Mao Tse-Tung!" [1]

"This is no godless Communist!" the sister responded, horrified.

So it's possible that my sacramental life began that day in Spohn Hospital.

It's true that from the beginning I had an affinity for nuns. Some two years later we returned to Spohn for my brother's birth, and one of my earliest memories dates to this time. I became angry with my father for some reason, and like any 3-year-old, I ran away. My father found me ensconced with the nuns, happily eating candy and being generally admired and petted affectionately. I don't remember what happened after that!

Perhaps because of these early encounters, I used to play at being a nun in a vague way. I used to wrap a blue blanket around my head like a veil, and whenever I played "bride" with my friends I decided my spouse would be God. God and I had a good relationship and it seemed natural to me to want to marry Him.

---

1.   Mao Tse-Tung was the leader of Communist China in 1971, when I was born.

We walked together in the backyard in the cool of the evening (just like in Genesis!) and I sang Him songs and hymns. Our church had a wall separating the fellowship hall into two sections, and for some reason the wall had windows with thick curtains set in it. This convinced me as a little girl that people lived in our church permanently, spending all their time with God, and I decided that when I grew up and married God I would live in the church, too. A movie like *The Sound of Music* threw me first into raptures—these women lived in church with God, too!—then into disgust when I realized Maria was going to leave the cloister and marry Captain von Trapp. For the same reason, I loved *The Trouble with Angels*, where the most troublesome girl in school ends up hearing the call and becoming a nun.

Now, had I been a Catholic, all of this would have been very normal. But I was raised a Christian Scientist, and no one knew quite what to do with me. There was no monastic outlet in our faith, and no way of consecrating yourself to God, even as a minister or a missionary. It seemed clear to me at a young age that Christian Science was not the faith for me. But, although I was attracted to the Catholic faith, I was a little frightened of it, too. I looked at all kinds of faiths, Christian and non-Christian, but nothing seemed to satisfy my longing. Finally, one day I attended Mass with my Girl Scout troop. I was 11, and the whole experience shook me tremendously. I had a strong feeling that someday I would return to this church, St. Raphael's, and indeed I did. Thirteen years later I was received into the Catholic Church at St. Raphael's, April 15, 1995.

When I was 12, I made the mistake of confiding to my lab group in science class the fact that I entertained hopes of someday being a nun. Why I did this, I'll never know, because word spread all over the junior high and overnight I became a social pariah. Frantically, I sought to repair the damage by being as "un-nun-like" as possible, dressing like a popular singer of the day, reading romantic novels, and giggling at boys. Yet in my heart I couldn't quite give up the dream, and occasionally I turned it over in my mind. But how would it ever be realized? I decided when I was in high school that if God really wanted me to be a nun, He would let me know somehow. One thing I never gave up was reading the Bible and praying every day, and I often went to the Christian Science church, although I had many difficulties with it. Finally, I went off to college, putting all my energies into a major in music and a minor in Russian.

I promised my parents I would contact a Christian Science group at the college, and through the workings of Divine Providence, that group set me on the wobbly course I followed through my adulthood to the cloister. One of the faculty leaders of the group was a music professor and also an expert in Russian, and she took me to services at an Orthodox church around Christmas of my sophomore year in college. The service entranced me … the singing, the prostrations, the kissing of icons and lighting of candles … *this* was the way to worship God! After the holidays, I became a catechumen, and I was finally baptized later that year, on December 8, 1991. I remained a member of this church for a couple of years and was very happy. I even considered becoming an Orthodox nun. Then in 1992, I went to Russia on a summer program. Ironically, it was in Russia, where I was surrounded by Orthodoxy, that I realized God had called me to be a Catholic. Even now it's hard for me to explain this, because I love the Orthodox Church, and I suppose I could have become a Maronite Catholic if I wanted to have the best of both worlds. But I felt then—as I feel now—that God was calling me to live the faith of my ancestors, who were all solidly Western-rite Catholics from Scotland and southern Germany. When I came home, I began reading anything I could get my hands on that dealt with Catholicism—so my reading was at times a little random! But the Holy Spirit protected me from heresy, and the worst confusion I got into was easily solved in the confessional.

In 1995, I was finally received into the Catholic Church. About this time, I also began teaching in an inner city school, and things were very difficult—drugs, gang activity, students being killed, all kinds of horrors. Still, I wondered if God were perhaps calling me to a life of service in this way. In fact, I had applied to enter an active Order and decided at the last minute not to enter because of this dilemma. However, the longer I taught, the more I felt that only prayer, sacrifice, and reparation would help my students and all the people I encountered on a daily basis. More and more I was drawn to the cloistered life. At last I decided I would never be happy unless I gave it a serious try. Reading the *Dialogue* of St. Catherine of Siena had convinced me that the Dominican Order was the one for me, and providentially there was a Dominican monastery in Texas. Although I professed willingness to leave my native state, I secretly hoped to stay in Texas … so this seemed very promising! I came for a visit in September, made a short aspirancy in December-January, and entered the day after school finished, May 27, 2000. I have never been happier than I have been in the cloister! God is truly great and wonderful in all His works!

Sister Mary Augustine on her golden jubilee

Our Lady's Gift

Sister Mary Augustine of the Passion, O.P.
Syracuse, NY

During World War II, I had joined the WAVE's but after three years of service in the Navy, I embarked on another adventure in civilian life: I worked with the U.S. Government in Germany, first as a secretary and then as an interpreter with the European Command Intelligence School at Oberammergau in the Bavarian Alps. My work there was exciting: I interpreted for displaced persons searching for opportunities to find a new life in the United States. I was in Oberammergau for four years, able to enjoy mountain climbing, skiing, and traveling. There was a wonderful journey to Rome during summer vacation and an audience with Our Holy Father Pius XII at Castel' Gandolfo.

In one of our military newspapers, a small one-inch ad announcing a pilgrimage to Lourdes caught my eye, and it tugged at my heart until I realized that I had to make that pilgrimage. Taking advantage of some vacation leave, I embarked on the journey after catching up with the pilgrims in Frankfurt. An Army chaplain was conducting the pilgrimage, which included some wheelchair patients hoping to be favored with a cure. We arrived in Lourdes late in the evening. My first desire was to go to the Grotto, so although it was late my traveling companion and I ran down there and knelt in prayer. The holiness and peace of the Grotto and the surrounding area was powerful. I was praying for people in general, family, friends, and so on, but it never occurred to me to pray for a religious vocation. After praying for a long time we proceeded to leave the Grotto, and my friend asked me if I knew what *he* was praying for. He then told me he felt he had a calling to the priesthood. I looked at him with awe, and wondered how it felt to have a "calling." Little did I know that Our Blessed Mother had planted the seed of a religious vocation in my heart, something I didn't realize until after my return to Oberammergau.

Back in the town, I experienced a complete change in my lifestyle: my party days were over, and all I had done before the pilgrimage seemed superficial. My only desire was to pray and although I prayed the rosary every day, I was drawn deeper into prayer and found my way to the village church each morning, even in the deep snow. My new gift of praying and spiritual searching continued, and I realized that the Holy Spirit was drawing me into a mystical life of prayer. I decided to quit my job and return to the States.

After I arrived home, I enrolled in a course of studies at Marywood College in Scranton, Pennsylvania intending to pursue a degree in languages at Fordham University. While in Scranton, however, I had a persistent desire to attend a weekend retreat at the Villa of Our Lady of the Poconos. During the retreat I prayed insistently for direction, and in desperation asked Our Lady, "Okay, dear Blessed Mother, now what do you want me to do? It's not what I want; but what do *you* want?" The Holy Spirit penetrated my entire being with a profound desire to enter a convent. When I returned from the retreat my college roommate detected a great change in me and asked what was happening. I told her about my desire to enter a convent, and she asked me to what type of religious life I felt drawn. "I just want to pray," I replied. She said she knew of the nicest Dominican cloister in Syracuse, upstate New York.

After a visit there for an interview with the prioress, I felt so completely at home that I had no desire to leave. On March 25, 1954, Feast of the Annunciation, I entered the Dominican Monastery of the Perpetual Rosary. On August 28, 2004, I celebrated my 50th Jubilee in the monastery and continue to serve God Our Father, Our Lord Jesus, and the Holy Spirit with a spirit of fidelity and grateful love in my golden years of religious life.

Mary's Tale

Sister Mary of the Incarnation, O.P.
Bronx, NY

As I sort through my memories of growing up, entering religious life, living these 40 plus years in different places and doing a variety of ministries, I am struck with the overwhelming sense of God's provident presence.

My tenth year stands out as being critical in my decision to become a sister. It was the year my father firmly, but lovingly, tried to explain to me why a girl could never replace Phil Rizzuto as the Yankee shortstop. Even though I was initially disappointed, it opened me up to the possibility that maybe God was calling me to be like my other hero, my 5th grade teacher. Sister James Dolores was young, pretty, and dynamic. She had insisted from the beginning that her students learn to pray and not just say prayers. She encouraged us to make frequent visits to the Blessed Sacrament and the Blessed Mother, to talk to them and listen. Often, she shared with us her own convictions and insights regarding religious life. When I enthusiastically told my parents that I was going to be a sister they reverted to the "we'll see" mode. I said no more until the 8th grade when I chose a small girl's high school, because I felt attracted to the opportunities they offered in the spiritual and apostolic life. They also had a good reputation for academics and sports. My parents said they were considering the better-known schools and they suggested a visit with my godmother, a Visitandine who had gone to school with my mother. The visit was both challenging and affirming. Sister said that the life of a nun was a demanding and disciplined one. She continued that my parents thought I was much too young to be thinking about being a nun, and they saw my choice of St. Clare's as part of my "nun plan." Sister Emmanuel said that she disagreed that I was too young but I could show them my maturity by committing myself to the Nine First Fridays at the monastery. So, once a month I made the 45-minute jaunt after school and prayed with the nuns for one and a half hours. I made 17 months until a bout with strep throat kept me in bed. My parents said no more and I began high school. The four years were a wonderful experience of challenging courses, supportive relationships, and strong service-oriented religious studies. The Sodality and the Legion of Mary kept me aware of the less fortunate, but the emphasis on communal vocal prayer left me with a conundrum. Time became an oppressor. Studies, sports, ministry, sharing a room, and—perhaps most telling—a teenager's abhorrence of being different kept me from going off as I used to, to pray. During the summers, which were spent at the beach, I could go off for long walks and be quiet with God. I saw Sister Emmanuel less frequently. In retrospect, I am in admiration of her patience and perseverance in praying for me and listening as I regaled her with our Catholic Action successes and shared my growing admiration of the Franciscan Sisters who taught us and worked side by side with us in the hospitals and orphanages where we volunteered. As senior year began and our class shared dreams and hopes for the future, it became clear that seven of us would be entering religious life. However, while the Franciscans accepted me, my beloved Classics teacher let me know that my years of being the "class clown" and a "little too opinionated" were raised with the Council at the time of the vote. I promised to be good.

The first 18 months in the novitiate were a special time of growth and deepening. My Novice Mistress, Sister Anne Roberta, let me know in no uncertain terms that she saw undeveloped potential in me, buried under layers of façade. She chipped and chiseled, hammered and cut. Sometimes I felt bruised and bloodied but never broken. At the end of the canonical year, everyone in my group went off to Fordham to begin their studies for certification as teachers. I went back to the kitchen pleased with the probability that I would be going to nursing school. Five months later, Sister sent for me to say that I was being "missioned" to a parish school to teach 5th grade. I was disappointed but strangely elated, scared but somehow confident. Sister looked deeply into my heart for what seemed like forever. Finally, she said, "It will never go easy for you, my child. Read and ponder John 21:15-19."

Life as a junior professed was stimulating and challenging. I even found that I enjoyed teaching. Since long holidays were spent at the novitiate, Holy Thursday found me arriving while the others were still at prayer, so I went into the community room. I was shocked to see my beloved Novice Mistress, obviously critically ill, trying to eat some lunch. I just stood there with tears pouring down my cheeks looking at her. Finally, she smiled a slow, sad smile and said, "You are hungry, child; go and eat." I never saw her again. She was hospitalized and died two weeks after my first vows.

Three years later, one of the nuns who had taught me was elected Mother General. She was not my choice, but I wasn't worried. I was having success in the classroom, I was doing well at Fordham and I felt loved and appreciated in my local community. The night before the ceremonial renewal of vows, each of us had a short visit with Mother General to ask for permission to renew our vows. My visit and the events that followed changed my life. I was vaguely aware of being uncomfortable as I entered, but when she said, "Sister, I'm not sure you will ever really change, so I need to think about granting you permission to renew your vows." My entire world just collapsed. As I left the room and walked down the corridor toward the student chapel I cried and cried. I had no words to say or ideas of what to do. My emptiness and sense of loss left me feeling naked and very much alone. After some time, I "knew" that a vocation is a gift from God. Our response to that gift must be ongoing. I owned whatever I had done to fail in my response, convinced that the God who had called me would always be faithful. Slowly I came to an inner awareness of why Sister Anne Roberta had given me John 21:15-19 as my device. "Do you love me enough to surrender your categories and concepts—the fallacy that salvation can be earned? Will you profess your love by following Me without reservation?" Peace followed and the conviction that I had been chosen by God and that He would show me the next step. I did renew my vows, made Final Profession in 1965, and a most interesting ministry challenge followed in 1966.

As a result of a review of our original studies requests, a new Mother General asked a few of us who were teaching to consider nursing. After a brief hesitation, I enthusiastically agreed. I had no idea then how demanding the science courses would be for this History Major, nor in my naïveté was I aware of how profoundly my life would be affected by the winds of change following Vatican II. Kathryn Sullivan, RSCJ, the scripture scholar, began a course for the mother-house community. As the youngest, I had the joy of driving her back and forth. These trips forged a special bond between us resulting in her request that I be able to live with the Religious of the Sacred Heart of Jesus while I finished my nursing studies. Away from the noise and expectations for help at the day nursery, I flourished academically. After graduation in 1969, I began work as a staff nurse at a Franciscan hospital. During that year, the number leaving the Franciscans increased dramatically. I was sad; but their agenda was not mine. I was reveling in my nursing and the Scripture courses I was taking with Sister Kathryn Sullivan. In 1971, having returned to graduate school, I was told by the Franciscan Mother General to consider seriously transfering as she could see no future for the Franciscans. Having lived 15 happy years as a Franciscan, I formally transferred to the Religious of the Sacred Heart, grateful for the opportunity to continue my life with these women whom I had come to esteem. Following my transition year, during which I studied the constitutions and spirituality of the Society under the mentorship of Sisters Margaret Williams and Ursula McAghon, I began teaching nursing and working part time in the Emergency Room. It was in this year that our province was visited by the Mother General from Rome. At dinner, while visiting our small community, she asked, "How many of you are willing to serve in the Third World?" All of our hands went up and I was gone six weeks later. I was not prepared for Africa but I was full of enthusiasm after the initial shock. Surely God was asking me to give up the ego satisfaction of my community and nursing ministry. "Do you love me more than these?" … "Follow me!" I arrived. There were plenty of sick but no dispensary, medicine, nor money. The bishop said, "Raise the money," (but not how). The Mother General said she would help (but not when). The East African Provincial said, "Forget it, I could use you as a secondary teacher" (to which I said, "No"). The dispensary was finally built by the people; medicine was obtained from other missionaries; babies were born and the sick cared for, but I had failed: failed to continue seeking clarification of my mandate, in assuming that in this international province international support (Mother General sent me a Land Rover) equaled provincial approval. I came home after three years, and my American provincial kindly blamed my problems on a lack of international experience. After a vacation, I eagerly plunged into Intensive Care nursing, living in the provincial house community where communication did not require constant interpretation. Eventually, God would use the African disappointment to open my heart to another international experience.

A Roman sabbatical was a real surprise since I was slated for the Philippines Renewal Group: another series of events and circumstances, not of my choosing, but certainly meant to convince me that "all things work together unto good for them that love God." As a special treat, I was sent to Assisi for a week with my RSCJ spiritual director before the renewal program began. Assisi was unencumbered space and time. We shared, walked the Umbrian hills, and prayed the Liturgy of the Hours with the Poor Clares. When the Renewal Program opened on February 1, the input, times for prayer, and the silence continued to nourish my hunger. On February 13, an RSCJ of the Italian province was struck by a car. The accident left her severely injured and deeply comatose. We prayed for her, but none of us knew her. Sunday I was up early so I had breakfast "in Italian" with the house community. One of the sisters said to me, "Please help our Sister Sophie. Sister Williams said you are a nurse." I understood their words even though I didn't want to … Selfishly I began to search my limited Italian vocabulary for excuses. I wanted this nun with the searching eyes to understand my limitations of language, a lack of credentials in Italy, etc. I hoped she couldn't see my selfishness. After all, I was on a sabbatical for spiritual renewal and I needed it. In the end I was too ashamed to say anything but yes.

The bus ride across Rome, the problem communicating, the horror of finding Sister Sophie three days after the accident unwashed with the blood and mud of the road still caked on her body—all this contributed to my conviction that someone should do something. I spoke to the local superior, the provincial, the director of the Renewal Program. Basically they all said the same thing: that her injuries were incompatible with life so the hospital had given her low priority and the local community (all retired) was doing its best to provide "sitters." I was totally and completely frustrated, and feeling absolutely helpless. I continued to take my "shift" on my free day and taught the other "sitters" some basic nursing care. This led to many laughs as I struggled to express myself in Italian. My renewal program was excellent but Sister Sophie dominated my prayer and reflection. Slowly a question formed that would eventually re-focus my life. "Can you stand beneath the cross with Mary and take the dead Christ in your arms?" Little did I know that this was only a beginning. A series of small miracles followed and over the next 10 months Sister Sophie was restored to her community. I still had a lot of learning to do.

On Holy Thursday, I was kneeling before the Repository trying to do my *lectio* on Peter's confrontation with the servant girl in the High Priest's house. I was in the community's chapel surrounded by the old and the sick. Peter/I said, "I'm not one of these." Peter/I was on the spot. It was a moment of truth. How far into the mystery of suffering was I willing to go? Like Peter, I was frightened, but I stayed with the question until slowly it became clear. What I had naively considered coincidences were really the movements of grace calling me into a beginning awareness of the implications of belonging to the Body of Christ. Our lives are inter-connected. God asks us to exchange burdens as well as graces; to be open enough to give or receive, to listen and to wait.

When I began teaching in the Intensive Care Unit, the focus was on the critically ill person and the family. Within 10 years there was a significant change in the curriculum from the person to the machine. The care and maintenance of the computers that were suppose to free the nurse to spend more time with the patient proved just the opposite. I decided that I needed to find a more person-centered form of nursing. At that time, I received an offer for a Geriatric Nurse Practitioner course for faculty. I jumped at the opportunity. In exchange for a short interlude as instructor, I was able to qualify in a year to take the national certifying exam and so I was launched on a happy, productive 13 years in the

Sacred Heart infirmaries. There the experience of Holy Thursday in Rome came to fruition as I managed the care of our own sisters, and had the privilege of walking in friendship with a few of them as they prepared for eternal life. I count it a special blessing that God used me as an instrument of grace for these friends. I know it opened up dimensions of my life and service that prepared me for my contemplative vocation.

One cold winter's night, we had a call from the nearby monastery asking to borrow a piece of medical equipment. I was asked to deliver it and demonstrate its use. I arrived and was greeted warmly. As I finished my explanation I was aware of a deep peace, and God's presence was almost palpable. I didn't want to leave and the sisters graciously asked me to have a hot drink. When I left that night a part of my heart remained behind. I began attending Vespers and making a Holy Hour on Sundays and would stop by on my way home for a visit. I asked one of the sisters if she would see me regularly to discuss my life and my prayer. She graciously accepted and a deep friendship was begun. As time went by, I became aware of a stirring deep within me, a strong attraction to the contemplative life. I sought advice from those who knew me best with the Religious of the Sacred Heart, and slowly it became clear to me and anyone who knew me well that it was real. My contemplative friend kept a very low profile, when she wasn't trying to discourage me. I made a retreat in the springtime of that year and knew at its conclusion that God was calling me at the age of 55, with Parkinson's Disease, to be a Dominican contemplative. I entered at the end of November 1995, made Solemn Profession in December 2001. I have made the prayer of Dag Hammarskjold my own, "For all that has been thanks, for all that shall be yes." (Dag Hammarskjold, *Markings*)

Sister Michael Marie as a postulant in 1943

God or Summer School

Sister Michael Marie Cygrymus, O.P.
Lancaster, PA

For me, it all started as I was leaving church services one day, when Father Henry Podowski, a holy priest whom I much admired, accosted me and said, "I want you to make a retreat." "When?" I asked. He told me the date and I quickly responded that I could not, as I had already signed up for summer school. Father looked somewhat perplexed and inquired, "You didn't flunk?" I quickly responded, "No, I want to make high school in three years." He said, "Is it going to be God or summer school?" I had no alternative but to accept the invitation.

The retreat was a full week preached by Father Louis Farina, an exceptionally holy man. It was a tremendous experience for me, never having previously made a retreat. On the very first day we were given a copy of the New Testament and when Father quoted Scripture he waited until all the retreatants located the passage. Thus began my love for the Bible and it has increased ever since. After the retreat I asked Father Podowski to be my spiritual director, as I learned almost all making the retreat had a spiritual director. He readily agreed. The following day I received a copy of St. Francis de Sales's *Introduction to a Devout Life*, which I devoured but did not always understand. I began to attend daily Mass and started to live an ascetic life. To my confessor's amazement, I rose around 4:00 a.m. to pray. He almost went through the grate at my next confession and exclaimed, "I never meant for you to rise that early. I only wanted you to be on time for Mass." I sometimes came late for one Mass but always stayed for the next that usually followed.

My paternal grandmother lived two streets away from us and we visited her almost daily. Since she was widowed quite young my father always looked out for her and frequently did maintenance work in her house. One particular day, Mrs. Kwitowski, our Sister Mary Columba's mother, was visiting and I understood enough Polish to know she was telling a hard luck story. She was accustomed to visit Sister Columba yearly and this would be the first year without a visit. The war was on and her daughter was working in a defense factory and for the first time would not be able to accompany her. I quickly ran up the hill to ask my mother if I could take her—I thought it would be great to see the capital of Pennsylvania! (Our first provisional monastery was across the river from Harrisburg.) My mother said, "How are you going to go to Harrisburg, when she can't speak English and you can't speak Polish?" My reply was that we weren't walking, and all that was needed was directions from her daughter. My mother gave in and let me go. I found out later that Sister Columba's mother knew I had a religious vocation and wanted to introduce me to the Order.

So off we went, she to see Sister Columba and I to see the capital.

When we arrived in Harrisburg, we took a local bus to South Enola where the monastery was located. On the front entrance to the monastery was a sign *Ring Bell and Walk In*. We did, and it was a terrific experience: the door to the chapel was just a few feet away and it was open. We heard the nuns chanting the Divine Office; it was ethereal. I'd never heard nuns chant before and I was enamored.

There was a Passionist monastery at the top of our hill, and many churches and schools where sisters taught, but meeting Dominicans was an exciting experience. I immediately fell in love with the Dominican spirit. Sister Columba and all the others were so totally dedicated and unassuming. I wanted to become part of it.

Sister Columba's mother and I stayed two nights, and I was determined to come back and stay forever. I requested and filled out an application for admission. Mother Mary of the Immaculate Heart knew my mother and dad through correspondence, and she and the members of the Council recognized that I had a vocation. It was really not on the spur of the moment: I had always had a deep conviction that I was called to be a nun. My mother confided to me years later that when I was born she had prayed that if God wanted it, she would like to see me a nun.

As soon as I got home, I told my mother that I applied for admission and was accepted. Mother calmly said, "When you are 21, no sooner!" I knew it would be impossible to get around my mother and so off to Dad I went. His response was, "What kind of stupid, idiotic nun are you going to be if you quit school?" I assured him Dominicans study and I would have five years of it in the novitiate. To make a long story short, my father spoke to my spiritual director who assured my dad that he knew I had a religious vocation, but expected that I would be around for some years. He suggested that my parents permit me to enter and if it was God's will it would last, if not I would be back home. My dad convinced my mother that the sooner she let me go, the sooner I would be back home and over these crazy ideas ... wait till they give her carrots to eat! I entered the South Enola monastery on September 12, 1943. The very next day, a bushel of carrots was donated and one of my first jobs was to peel them!

Many years have gone by and I have studied. Mother Mary of the Immaculate Heart Ricco, originally from the Union City monastery, was our prioress for many years. She was a true lover of everything Dominican, and saw to it that we regularly had lectures and music teachers. I learned and studied much under her, and I know my dad was pleased. I have been sacristan, procuratrix, bursar, infirmarian, novice mistress, and prioress.

Deo Gratias.

My Vocation Story: No Secrets

Sister Marie Tersidis, O.P.
Lufkin, TX

I grew up in East Africa. It was in 1977 that my vocation to religious life began to stir. I was born and raised around religious. My schoolteachers were 80 percent religious sisters. Besides, I have an older sister who is a religious. Providentially, our home is very close to the motherhouse of my sister's religious community so I had the privilege of attending daily Mass at the convent before school for seven years from the age of 10 to 17.

My love for the sisters grew. Their singing and their habit, which always looked so clean, fascinated me. Above all, their prayer life was uplifting. I can recall one highlight at the convent was the Corpus Christi procession when the little girls threw flowers at Jesus as the priest carried him around the convent. This procession lasted at least three hours and yet it seemed like minutes. The memory of this solemn occasion has never left my mind.

As I grew, observing the sisters coming to Mass in procession after their morning prayers and making their profound genuflection on both knees two by two, made my heart dance with joy. I could hardly wait to be one of them. At school I volunteered to help the sisters carry their bags and clean their dining room, etc., but that was not enough. I just knew I wanted to be like them in a fuller sense.

As soon as I completed elementary school, I sought to enter the convent, but by this time I did not want to join the community that my sister belonged to. I chose an international congregation, which meant I had to learn English. I did well with English. However, as I advanced in my religious training, I faced a challenge that threw me off my horse. The senior sisters who returned from their missionary activities shared with the novices their experiences in the missions. The spirit of the founder was to preach the Word to all people and especially to the people in the remotest parts of the world. There are parts of the world where education is unheard-of, and people are really primitive in many ways—clothing and eating, to mention a few. Now, one of the challenges at the missions was to identify with the people in their way of eating and dressing. I could not see myself dressed in beads or animal skin! That was way too difficult for me to conceive. I was too afraid to face this reality so I chose to go back home and pursue high school studies.

At this time, my interest in religious life vanished. I did not want anything to do with religious life. I even developed a strong aversion towards the sisters at school. I did not want anything that would associate me with religious although, for some reason, when one lives in the convent long enough one begins to behave somewhat like sisters. For instance, I could not miss morning Mass and frequent confession. Some of the students found that too much and they called me "Sister," which annoyed me.

I tried to silence the voice within me. I thought I had succeeded when all of a sudden, the final year of my studies, the desire came back stronger than ever. I was ashamed to tell anybody because I had been attending some social activities, not evil by any means, but according to my culture and the mentality of my people, anyone aspiring to become a religious should keep away from dancing, cinemas or having boyfriends, etc.

Now the dance changed. It was no longer an outward dance, but an inward dance of the heart. The Lord beckoned me with melodies far beyond human enticements. I had now to face the reality that I could no longer quench the desire to consecrate my life to God. It felt so unreal and yet so real. A mixed feeling! I started asking advice. My parish priest did not seem convinced of my vocation. This was very painful, but I trusted in God. Finally, I decided to go back to the same community I left. I thought, "I was a coward. If others can make it, why can't I?"

I was accepted the second time. I was full of confidence and very determined to persevere. I can remember telling myself, "It is now or never." Not too long after my entrance a big temptation swept over me. The results of my high school exam came out and I had passed and the government had offered me a teaching diploma course with a sizeable stipend. Grace triumphed. I gave it up. I have never regretted this decision because had I pursued higher studies, I am not sure I would be here.

I applied myself to my religious training. Two years passed. Then my fears about the missions began to build up. I could not believe I was to step out of the convent a second time.

My father was very happy about the whole drama because he did not want me to become a sister. He considered religious life a lazy state of life and an unfortunate way of life. He could not reconcile the fact that his daughters would one day die having no children to anoint their foreheads. He was in ecstasy when I started looking into other states of life. At this point, I was convinced I wanted to be a nurse and eventually a doctor. I applied to a pre-nursing school. My first year in the dispensary, I was assigned to the labor ward. I got sick at the third delivery. That ended my nursing vocation.

And now, what next? What a dilemma! What a disappointment! I was plunged into a dense cloud where I was drawn to pray and to meditate on the word of God. I had within me the faith to seek the will of God in my life at any cost. My family was very mad at me because I had given up what was "the most important in the world," namely education and the good jobs that go with it. My parish priest pleaded with the government to reconsider my chance for the diploma course. It was too late. I was happy he did not succeed because I had completely turned my mind away from that direction. I was being led by the light of faith amid thick darkness.

Finally, the Lord, in his own mysterious way, led me to my true vocation. This I cannot explain because I never wanted to become a cloistered nun. I had heard a lot of strange stories about nuns with their instruments of discipline, the coffin under the bed, etc. I was scared even at the mere mention of the name "monastery." Providentially, I was acquainted with a Dominican priest who wanted to establish a contemplative religious community in his country in West Africa. The priest was a good friend of the Dominican nuns in Lufkin, Texas, U.S.A. He managed to convince me that nuns live a normal life and that I should come to the States to be trained so that I could be of help in the formation of those interested in the life back in Africa.

I came to Lufkin and met the nuns. I was so scared that my neck hardly moved. I looked at them so carefully. I noticed they were happy. They dressed the same. There was nothing that indicated different classes in the way they dressed. Then, I was led to the enclosure where I awaited strange things to happen. Nothing extraordinary happened. I noticed, too, they ate from the same table with the prioress and did everything in a good community spirit. I began to feel at home and at peace. I began to realize and savor the nobility of the life.

Before I knew it, my time for training was over and I had to go back to Africa to help in the formation of the postulants and novices. There I met another disappointment. The original vision of the community had changed remarkably within the two years I was away. I was trained to live Dominican contemplative life, which, unfortunately, was no longer practiced in the young community. I realized then that my real vocation was to be a cloistered contemplative after all. I sought to come back to Lufkin, and here I am.

All I had to do was to say yes to God, try it out, and let God do His work. I felt like Peter and the apostles when they spent all night fishing with no success. When the Lord gave the command to cast the net into deep water they caught more than they could handle. The same could be said of my vocation story. The Lord let me try so hard with no success until he plunged me into the enclosure.

From Here to Eternity: a Thumbnail Sketch

Sister Maria-Agnes Karasig, O.P.
Summit, NJ

Sponsabo te mihi in fide (*I will espouse you to me in faith*) was the motto inscribed on my profession ring when I pronounced my perpetual vows of poverty, chastity, and obedience in the Congregation of Dominican Sisters of St. Catherine of Siena, Philippines. It was the last day of May in 1961 and some of the distilled radiance of my espousal in faith with Christ has been captured in black and white photos that I kept in an album. After profession, religious life continued its rhythm of prayer, community, study, and apostolate. Obedience would send me to teach music, English Literature, Spanish, and theology in various high schools and colleges located in far flung islands—Palawan, Jolo, Samar—and the mountainous region of Cagayan. Unexpected appointments—registrar, treasurer, librarian, sacristan, choir directress, superior of a small community and administrator of a college—would test my resilience and empty out all my resources. It was always yes to my Spouse in faith. It had been a professionally fulfilled life. But my heart was deeply hollowed by the unsatisfied yearning for the cloistered contemplative life.

On my last retreat at the Motherhouse in 1973, I looked back with gratitude and nostalgia at the ways and means by which God had called me to live a life of intimate union with Him as a vowed religious. I was the oldest of five children in a mixed marriage, my mother being a devout Catholic and my father a liberal Protestant. After trying different Protestant churches and sampling current schools of thought I ended up a Methodist. Then, at the University of Santo Tomas in Manila, God called me to live the fullness of Christian life by becoming a Catholic. Father Adolfo Garcia, O.P., then provincial of Holy Rosary Province, baptized me on December 9, 1953 at the U.S.T. chapel. After that, I joined the Legion of Mary and Catholic Action. The waters of baptism and the Holy Spirit had implanted in my soul the seed of a religious vocation. I visited the Carmelites and the Pink Sisters, but their vibes did not resonate with the desire of my heart. Intermediate causes (as St. Thomas puts it) led me to the Order of Preachers. Eleven months after my baptism I entered the convent in 1954. Entrance dates are beyond forgetting; the tearful goodbyes, farewell parties, the last movie, the last concert, best wishes and regrets expressed by friends and relatives. There were material things to be disposed of, and the once treasured memorabilia—worldly photos, love letters, Valentine cards, roses and orchids pressed in the pages of a book—must now be consigned to the fire. Ah! The holocaust of memories!

That last retreat at the Motherhouse was also a preparation for my transfer to the Monastery of Our Lady of the Rosary in Summit, New Jersey, U.S.A. Way back in 1962, I discovered the Summit monastery in a book written by Mother Mary Aloysius, O.P. on the history of the Dominican Sisters of the Perpetual Rosary. With the blessing but reluctant permission of our Mother General I wrote a letter of application to transfer to the Summit monastery, but was denied admission. The Archbishop of Newark cautioned the Mother Prioress not to accept transfer candidates from foreign countries of different cultures. Eleven years would elapse before the renewal of my application would be accepted favorably by the Council and Chapter of the monastery. On August 2, 1973, I signed the rescript of transfer issued by the Sacred Congregation in the presence of my spiritual director, Father Pablo Fernandez, O.P. There were heart-wrenching goodbyes with my natural family and my congregation. The emotional amputation was complete. I entered the Summit monastery on August 4, 1973 as a transfer candidate (in fact, a perpetually professed novice) and I pronounced my solemn vows on March 19, 1977.

Deus cordis mei (*God of my heart*) is the personal motto inscribed on my profession ring. It sums up my Dominican monastic contemplative life, an undivided heart free for God alone and set apart as a hidden sanctuary of prayer for the world. Dominican itinerancy would call me out of Summit twice: first, to help begin the Philippine monastery at Cainta (1977-1980) and second, to serve there as a postulated prioress (2003-2006). Again, it was yes to the God of my heart. The poetry and theology written on vocation brochures and websites are concretized in the day-to-day prosaic duties in the monastery. Yes, it is a life of daily dying to self and rising to Christ. It is also a life filled with humor and laughter.

Why Summit? The Cross has a drawing power. It is here that I can deny myself more and practice the renunciations that are the hallmark of the life of a nun. It is here that I am called to authenticate and appropriate in my life the fruits of liturgy, study, prayer, and *lectio divina*, and to internalize the Rule and

Constitutions. It is in community that I can live the spirit of enclosure with flesh and blood humanity and not just with walls and grilles. Why Summit? Leave the rest of the answers to heaven. In the ultimate analysis, vocation is an inscrutable mystery.

Glossary

Albert the Great, Saint. (1206-1280) Dominican scholar, bishop, and Doctor of the Church. He was instrumental in reintroducing the works of Aristotle to the West. He taught Thomas Aquinas. The title "Great" was given him by his contemporaries in recognition of the extensiveness of his knowledge. He loved natural science, and is thus the patron of scientists.

active. Used to designate religious with active apostolates—nursing, teaching, social work, etc.

apostolate. Used here to specify the type of work done by different congregations or Orders for the spreading of the Gospel.

apostolic. In the context of this book, normally used as a synonym for **active**. Also, any activity that promotes the spreading of the Gospel.

ascetic. Comes from a Greek word for discipline. It means the performance of spiritual exercises for the purpose of acquiring virtue.

aspirancy. A period of time spent within the enclosure for the purpose of discernment by one aspiring to live the contemplative life.

Augustine, Saint. 354-430. Doctor of the Church. His writings have had a tremendous influence on the Western Church. He wrote the Rule which Dominicans and many other religious institutes follow.

Benedictine. A member of the ancient monastic Order founded by St. Benedict of Nursia in Italy in the 6th century.

Benediction. A solemn blessing by a priest or deacon with the Blessed Sacrament. A paraliturgical rite, it usually includes exposition, the singing of hymns, and the recitation of the Divine Praises.

bursar. The nun in charge of handling the community's finances and the temporal needs of the monastery. See also **procuratrix**.

C.P. Abbreviation for Congregation of the Passion. Commonly known as **Passionists**.

canon. A community of priests gathered about the bishop of a diocese at his cathedral, who celebrate the Divine Office. These priests usually live a contemplative life, although they might go out for priestly ministry. Most followed the Rule of St. Augustine.

canon law. Church law that governs all Roman Catholics.

Capuchin. A type of Franciscan.

Carmel. Name used to designate a Carmelite monastery referring to Mount Carmel in Palestine where the Carmelite Order was founded.

Carmelite. A member of the Carmelite Order founded for men in 1226 in Palestine. They became mendicant friars. Two hundred years later, contemplative nuns were affiliated to them. Often it refers to Discalced Carmelites, the reform of St. Teresa of Avila made in 1562, probably the most well-known of the contemplative Orders.

Catherine of Siena, Saint. 1347-1380. Lay Dominican, doctor of the Church, peacemaker. She was instrumental in bringing the Pope back to Rome from Avignon.

Catholic Action. Pope Pius XI defined Catholic Action as, "The participation of the Catholic laity in the apostolate of the hierarchy." It is various lay organizations who, with the mandate of the bishop and under his direction, work for the salvation of souls.

Chapter. The monastery Chapter is composed of all the perpetually professed members of the community. It decides matters of major importance for the monastery. The Chapter elects the prioress and members of the Council. It also votes on the admission of candidates to the postulancy, novitiate, temporary profession, and solemn profession.

charism. The particular grace or gift given to the founder of an Order or congregation and passed on to his or her spiritual descendants for the benefit of the entire Church, e.g. Franciscans—poverty; Dominicans—truth.

chastity. The right ordering of the sexual appetite. All Christians are called to the practice of this virtue according to their state of life. Religious take a vow of chastity, which is a voluntary renunciation of all sexual acts and intimacy proper to the married state.

choir. Refers both to the nuns gathered together for the recitation of the Liturgy of the Hours and to the physical room where they gather for it.

Cistercian. A reform of the Benedictines. Its most famous early member was St. Bernard of Clairvoux (1090-1153). The Order has both monks and nuns.

clerical. Having to do with the priesthood.

cloister. Refers to the area of the monastery reserved to the nuns, which is not ordinarily open to outsiders and from which the nuns do not ordinarily leave.

cloistered. Means that the nuns stay in one physical place and do not leave it.

communion railing. Before the reform of the liturgy after Vatican II, most churches had a communion railing separating the sanctuary from the rest of the Church. It was where the communicants knelt to receive communion. The communion railing is still maintained in some churches.

congregation. A group of religious bound by a rule who profess simple vows.

contemplative. Refers in this book to a way of life devoted primarily to prayer.

convent. A building where the regular life of a religious community is lived. Can refer to houses of both men and women. In the U.S. it is typically used to designate a house where sisters live.

Council. The monastery Council is a group of nuns under the presidency of the prioress whose advice or consent she is obliged to seek according to Dominican law. Normally there are four councillors or six if there are more than 20 professed nuns in the community. The subprioress, the novice mistress, and the nun who was prioress in the immediate preceding term are automatically on the Council. The rest are elected by the monastery Chapter.

Daughters of Charity. A congregation of active sisters renowned for nursing and teaching. Founded in France by St. Vincent de Paul in 1633; the first U.S. foundation was made by St. Elizabeth Ann Seton in 1809.

Daughters of the Heart of Mary. An active congregation of sisters founded in France in 1790.

Deo Gratias. Latin for "Thanks be to God."

Divine Office. Another name for the Liturgy of the Hours, the official prayer of the Church, which monks and nuns are bound to recite in its entirety.

Dominic, Saint. (1170-1221) Founder of the Order of Preachers. The youngest child of Felix de Guzmán and Blessed Jane of Aza. Born in Caleruega, Old Castile. His parents were of the lesser nobility. He followed his two older brothers into the priesthood, and was originally a cathedral canon at Osma before setting out with his bishop, Diego, on that fateful diplomatic mission.

Dominican Family. Used to describe all the different branches affiliated to the Dominican Order—nuns, friars, sisters, laity, youth, associates.

Dominican liturgy. Up until Vatican II, the Dominican Order had its own liturgical rite. At the time of its foundation, the celebration of the liturgy varied considerably from diocese to diocese. This caused much confusion when the friars gathered for their General Chapters. So the Order established a uniform liturgy to be observed by all Dominicans everywhere. It employed an older version of the Roman rite with less Frankish influences than the Tridentine rite (adopted by the universal Church after the Council of Trent). The chant used in the Dominican rite was mostly Cistercian chant simplified to facilitate time for study. The rite was known for its brevity.

Dominican Sister. A member of an active congregation of sisters affiliated with the Dominican Order. There are 23 congregations of the Third Order of St. Dominic in the U.S. Traditionally, teaching and nursing were their main apostolates. Now their fields of ministry are even more varied. Their origins are diverse. Some congregations were founded by Dominican friars. Others came from cloistered monasteries of Dominican nuns in Europe, who chose to teach in the U.S. because of the missionary needs of the time.

enclosure. The place reserved to the members of the monastery: the cloister. Also, the law governing entrance and egress from the cloister.

eremitic. Having to do with the life of a hermit. Certain Orders emphasize solitude and are called eremitic Orders.

evangelical counsels. The vows of poverty, chastity, and obedience—all recommended by Jesus in the New Testament for the perfection of charity. The public profession of these vows and life in common constitute religious life.

extern. An extern sister is one who is allowed to leave the enclosure to take care of guests and tend to other needs of the monastery. She does not take solemn vows, but perpetual simple vows. Each monastery writes its own rule for externs. The vocation of an extern sister is a specific calling. A person usually enters the monastery with the intention of becoming an extern. Before Vatican II, externs were not allowed to enter the enclosure. They lived on the outside. Now they are allowed to live inside the enclosure with the community. Since externs are not bound by enclosure they can attend events like vocation fairs and diocesan celebrations.

final vows. Vows taken for life. In the case of a nun these vows are solemn vows, in the case of a sister they are perpetual simple vows.

first vows. After the postulancy and novitiate, a period of about three years, temporary or "first" vows are taken for three years. These can then be renewed a year at a time, but the period of temporary profession can never exceed nine years. The person who takes them is bound under the vows for the period of time she has professed them. Although temporary, a person is considered a nun from the time she makes first vows. When the time of her vows expire she can either choose to make a perpetual commitment in solemn vows or leave the monastery.

Franciscan. A member of the Franciscan Order founded by St. Francis of Assisi in the 13th century in Italy.

friar. A member of a mendicant, or *begging*, Order. Friars are distinct from monks in that they do not remain within a monastery under the direction of an abbot. Their government is more centralized and their apostolate is in the world. Dominican men are not monks; they are friars. Other friars include Franciscans, Carmelites, Augustinians, Servites, Minims, Trinitarians, Mercedarians, the Order of Penance, and the Brothers of St. John of God.

Gregorian Chant. The official music of the Roman Rite. Sung in Latin, it was first written down in the 9th century and has been in continual use in the Church since then. Its origins are popularly ascribed to Pope Gregory the Great. The modern musical scale evolved from it.

grille. Usually an iron grating that physically separates the nuns from guests in the visiting parlors. Before Vatican II, it was required by the law of papal enclosure that all monasteries have a double grille. Although the double grille is retained in some places it is no longer a requirement of papal enclosure, but there must be a physical barrier between nuns and guests. For Dominican nuns this takes the form of a fixed counter or a simple grille.

habit. The distinctive religious garb worn by religious both to identify them as religious and the Order or congregation to which they belong. The habit of a Dominican nun is a white tunic with a belt and rosary attached, a white scapular and a black veil and cappa. (The cappa is a cape usually only worn for solemn occasions.)

Holy Cross Sisters. The teaching Sisters of the Holy Cross were founded in Le Mans, France in 1841 by Bl. Basil Anthony Moreau.

infirmarian. The nun in charge of the sick.

infirmary. The place in the monastery for the care of the sick.

Jesuit. A member of the Society of Jesus founded by St. Ignatius Loyola in 1540. Known for their schools. The society has no female branch.

lectio divina. Latin for "sacred" or "divine" reading, the monastic practice of reading the scriptures slowly and meditatively as addressed to oneself.

Legion of Mary. A confraternity founded in Dublin, Ireland, in 1921 by Frank Duffy. With three million members, it is the largest Catholic apostolic lay organization in the world. Members do door-to-door evangelization, visit parishioners and the sick and elderly.

Liturgy of the Hours. The official prayer of the Church. It is composed of the 150 Psalms spaced out over a month with readings from scripture and the Fathers of the Church. There are seven "hours" in the Liturgy of the Hours appointed to different times of the day in order to sanctify the whole day: Morning Prayer (*Lauds*), Midmorning Prayer (*Terce*), Midday Prayer (*Sext*), Midafternoon Prayer (*None*), Evening Prayer (*Vespers*), Night Prayer (*Compline*), and Office of Readings (*Matins*). Though called "hours" they do not usually take an hour to say. Some are quite short. Monks and nuns are obliged to recite the entire Liturgy of the Hours; priests and active religious: Morning and Evening Prayer, Daytime

Prayer and Night Prayer. All the Christian faithful are free to pray the Hours, and encouraged to do so. Dominican nuns are not only obliged to say the Hours, but to do so chorally in choir.

Magnificat. Mary's song of praise as recorded in Luke 1:46-55. It is sung daily during Evening Prayer.

Missionaries of Charity. A congregation of sisters founded by Bl. Teresa of Calcutta in 1950 to serve the poorest of the poor.

monastery. A residence of monks or nuns, usually including a chapel, chapter hall, refectory, private cells, and work area.

monastic. Having to do with a monastery or anything that pertains to the way of life of monks or nuns.

monk. A monk is a man who professes the evangelical counsels, lives apart from the world in a monastery with a community under an abbot. Monks, like nuns, are obliged to the entire recitation of the Liturgy of the Hours. Benedictines, Cistercians, Trappists, Carthusians, and Camaldolese are all monks.

monsignor. An honorary title given to a priest in recognition for his service to the Church.

monstrance. The vessel in which the Eucharistic host is placed for exposition of the Blessed Sacrament and for Benediction.

Mother. A form of address sometimes used for a prioress or superior of a community. At one time, it was also customary to address all the members of the Council as "Mother."

Mother General. The superior of a congregation of sisters.

Motherhouse. The main house of an active congregation of sisters where the formation usually takes place and where the Mother General resides as well as the retired sisters.

mystical. Having to do with mystery. The Christian faith is built on mysteries. To live a mystical life is to live a life according to faith, not on things apprehensible to the senses.

novice. A novice is a person who has completed the time of **postulancy** and still desires religious life. The novitiate usually lasts from one to two years. The habit of the Order is received sometime during this period.

novice mistress. The nun in charge of the training of the novices. She often has charge of all the women in training, including postulants and junior professed.

novitiate. This can refer to the building or section of the monastery reserved for the women in training, to the novices themselves, to the period of time one is a novice, or to everyone in training including postulants and junior professed. Dominicans nuns often refer to all who have not yet made final profession as "the novitiate."

nun. Strictly speaking, a nun is the female equivalent of a monk. Together with monks, nuns are obliged to the entire recitation of the **Liturgy of the Hours**. They have **solemn vows** and some form of **enclosure**. Normally, they do not engage in active apostlates, although some of the older Orders exercise the ministry of hospitality. In the U.S., "nun" is often used generically to refer to any female religious—active or contemplative.

O.P. Abbreviation for Order of Preachers, the official name of the Dominican Order.

papal enclosure. The rules of enclosure set out by the Holy See. Considered the most solemn form of enclosure, although individual Orders or monasteries can establish rules that are even stricter. Papal enclosure originated with Dominican nuns. Pope Honorius III asked St. Dominic to reform the nuns of Rome. The ones who were willing to reform gathered in the convent of San Sisto. Dominic, himself, carried the keys of the cloister, which he later entrusted to the Pope. In monasteries under papal enclosure, dispensations must be sought directly from Rome. Constitutional enclosure is that determined by the particular law of different religious institutes.

parlor. The room where the nuns meet with guests. For cloistered Dominicans there is either a simple grille or counter separating the nuns from the visitors.

Passionist. A member of the Congregation of the Passion founded by St. Paul of the Cross in 1720. A congregation made up of both priests and contemplative nuns, Passionists are particularly devoted to meditating on the Passion of Christ.

perpetual adoration. The practice of having the Blessed Sacrament exposed 24 hours a day with people taking turns for time of adoration in front of it.

Pink Sisters. Sister-Servants of the Holy Spirit of Perpetual Adoration. A contemplative congregation of sisters founded in Holland in 1896 by St. Arnold Janssen and Mother Mary Michaele. Called "Pink Sisters" for the distinctive pink habit they wear during adoration of the Blessed Sacrament.

Pius V, Saint. 1504-1572. Dominican pope who carried out the reforms of the Council of Trent, excommunicated Queen Elizabeth I, and saw the defeat of the Turks at the Battle of Lepanto. He established the feast of Our Lady of Victory, which was later changed to Our Lady of the Rosary.

Poor Clares. Order of St. Clare, contemplative nuns founded by St. Clare of Assisi, friend of St. Francis, in Italy in 1212.

postulant. The first stage of one who has entered a monastery or convent. It is a time of acclimation to religious life and preparation for the novitiate.

postulated. A nun is postulated when there are one or more impediments to her becoming prioress. For instance, if she has just served two consecutive three-year terms as prioress, if she is below 35, if she has not yet completed seven years from her solemn profession, or if she is from another monastery. Normally, a simple majority is required for the election of a prioress, but since postulations are usually only done in unusual circumstances or in case of real need a two-thirds majority is required for them.

prioress. Among Dominican nuns, a prioress is the superior of an individual monastery. She is elected by the solemnly professed members of the monastery for a three-year term. She can be re-elected for another immediate three-year term.

priory. A house for male religious governed by a prior. Dominican men only have priories; they do not have monasteries since they are not under an abbot.

procuratrix. The nun in charge of acquiring and caring for the temporal needs of the monastery. Also called **bursar.**

Redemptorist. A member of the Society of the Most Holy Redeemer, a congregation of priests and brothers founded by St. Alphonsus Liguori in Italy in 1732.

Known for their parish missions and work with the poor. There are also Redemptoristine nuns.

refectory. The room in the monastery where meals are taken.

registrar. A person in charge of keeping a register.

religious life. The way of life lived by persons who live in a community, have made a public profession of the evangelical counsels of poverty, chastity, and obedience, either **simple** or **solemn**, and follow a rule.

religious Order. A religious community where the members take **solemn vows**. It is also of some antiquity.

religious sister. A religious woman from a congregation where perpetual simple vows are taken. Usually refers to active religious, although there are some contemplative sisters who take perpetual simple vows, even some Dominicans.

RSCJ. The Society of the Sacred Heart; active religious sisters founded in France in 1800 by St. Madeleine Sophie Barat.

Sacred Congregation. The Congregation for Institutes of Consecrated Life and Societies of Apostolic Life—the Congregation in Rome that oversees religious life.

sacristan. The person who takes care of preparing the vessels, linen, vestments, and all the material things needed for the celebration of the liturgy.

silence. During the day, Dominican nuns are not supposed to be engaging in casual conversations with each other. They are allowed to speak briefly in matters pertaining to work. This is the rule of silence, which facilitates receptiveness to the Word of God and being able to extend one's prayer throughout the day. Silence is the atmosphere in which the Word speaks. Two times a day are allotted for conversation. These two periods are referred to as recreation. There are certain places in the monastery where silence is more strictly observed: in the Chapel, refectory, and dormitory. Also, the time after Compline (Night Prayer) until after Morning Prayer the next day is a time of solemn silence as well as the rest period in the afternoon.

Sister. Form of address used both for nuns and active women religious.

Sisters of St. Joseph. Active sisters founded in LePuy, France in 1650. There are 23 congregations of them in the U.S.

Sisters of the Atonement. Also known as Graymoor, it is a congregation of Franciscans, men and women, founded by Lewis T. Watson and Lurana White, both Episcoplians, in 1898. They were founded with the view of seeking union between Roman Catholicism and Anglicanism, and they were eventually received into the Roman Catholic Church.

Sodality of Mary. An association of the faithful for the promotion of devotion to Mary and acts of charity.

solemn vows. Solemn vows is the public perpetual profession made by a monk, nun, or any member of a religious Order of the evangelical counsels of poverty, chastity, and obedience. It is a more radical vow than the perpetual simple vows made by members of a religious congregation. It renders all acts, such as contracting marriage, not only illicit, but also invalid. With the solemn vow of poverty, the right to acquire and own anything is relinquished. The Dominican profession formula only mentions obedience, but poverty and chastity are understood to be included under it in the Constitutions.

spiritual director. A person, often a priest, who helps one discern what God is asking and where He is leading. As an experienced guide in the spiritual life, he or she can help bring objectivity to the situation.

spirituality. Spirituality is used in this book to refer to the particular way of approaching God specific to each religious institute. Similar to **charism.**

stalls. Choir stalls. The place in chapel assigned to each monk or nun for the chanting of the Liturgy of the Hours.

temporary vows. Vows taken for a temporary or specific period of time before solemn or perpetual profession.

Thérèse, Saint. 1873-1897. A Carmelite nun, doctor of the Church, patroness of the missions, who died in a French Carmel at the age of 24. Known to the world through her autobiography *Story of A Soul.* Probably the most famous cloistered nun of modern times.

Third Order. Laity who affiliate themselves with a religious Order to share in the spiritual benefits and charism of that Oder; also known as tertiaries. Franciscans, Dominicans, Premonstratensians, Carmelites, Benedictines, Augustinians, Servites, and Trinitarians all have Third Orders. Active religious sisters affiliated to an Order are called Third Order conventual, meaning they lead the regular life in common.

Thomas Aquinas, Saint. 1225-1274. Dominican, doctor of the Church. His teachings have been particularly recommended by the Church for study.

transfer. Going from one religious institute to another or from one monastery to another. Once transferred, the person is under the rule and leadership of the religious institute to which she has transferred.

Trappistines. Female branch of the Trappists (Cistercians of the Strict Observance). Founded in Citeaux, France in 1098. Contemplative nuns.

Trinitarian. Both priests and sisters of the Order of the Most Holy Trinity. Founded in France in 1198 by St. John De Matha for the ransom of Christian slaves.

veritas. Latin for "truth."

Vespers. Latin name for Evening Prayer in the Liturgy of the Hours. One of the principle prayers of the day.

Vincent Ferrer, Saint. 1350-1419. A Spanish Dominican famous for his preaching of the end times throughout Europe.

Visitandine. Nuns founded by St. Francis de Sales and St. Jane de Chantal in France in 1610. Some Visitandines are cloistered and others teach.

vocation. From the Latin *vocare*, "to call." All Christians have the universal call from God to holiness. Each individual is called to carry out that calling in a particular state of life: married, clerical, single, or religious. Everyone has a vocation to one of these states. The word is sometimes used to mean specifically the call to religious life.

List of English Speaking North American Monasteries of Dominican Nuns

Corpus Christ Monastery
1230 Lafayette Avenue
Bronx, NY 10474-5399
Phone: (718) 328-6996
Web: www.nunsopbronx.homestead.com
Email: vocationsbronx@verizon.net

Monastery of Our Lady of the Rosary
335 Doat Street
Buffalo, NY 14211-2199
Phone: (716) 892-0066

Monastery of the Perpetual Rosary
1500 Haddon Avenue
Camden, NJ 08103-3112
Phone: (856) 342-8340 or (856) 342-7462

Monastery of Mary the Queen
1310 West Church Street
Elmira, NY 14905-1998
Phone: (607) 734-9506
Web: www.op.org/maryqueen/
Email: elmiraop@localnet.com

Monastery of the Blessed Sacrament
29575 Middlebelt Road
Farmington Hills, MI 48334
Phone: (248) 626-8253

Web: www.opnuns-fh.org
Email: vocdir@sbcglobal.net

Monastery of the Immaculate Heart of Mary
1834 Lititz Pike
Lancaster, PA 17601-6585
Phone: (717) 569-2104
Email: monlanc@aol.com

Queen of Peace Monastery
9383 222nd Street
Langley, BC V1M 3T7
CANADA
Phone: (604) 513-3665
Email: peacenun@vcn.bc.ca

St. Dominic's Monastery
2636 Monastery Road
Linden, VA 22642
Phone: (540) 635-3259
Email: Lindenopnuns@aol.com

Monastery of the Angels
1977 Carmen Avenue
Los Angeles, CA 90068-4098
Phone: (323) 466-2186
Web: www.op-stjoesph.org/nuns/angels
Email: angels2@algxmail.com

Monastery of the Infant Jesus
1501 Lotus Lane
Lufkin, TX 75904-2699
Phone: (936) 634-4233
Web: www.lufkinnuns.op.org

Monastery of St. Jude
143 County Road 20, East
PO Box 170
Marbury, AL 36051-0170
Phone: (205) 755-1322

Web: www.stjudemonastery.org
Email: stjudemonastery@juno.com

Corpus Christi Monastery
215 Oak Grove Avenue
Menlo Park, CA 94025-3272
Phone: (650) 322-1801
Web: www.op.org/nunsmenlo

Our Lady of Grace Monastery
11 Race Hill Road
North Guilford, CT 06437-1099
Phone: (203) 457-0599
Web: www.op-stjoseph.org/nuns/olgrace/olgrace
Email: olgracevocations@juno.com

Monastery of Our Lady of the Rosary
543 Springfield Avenue
Summit, NJ 07901-4498
Phone: (908) 273-1228
Web: www.op.org/nunsopsummit
Email: vocations.summit@op.org

Monastery of the Perpetual Rosary
802 Court Street
Syracuse, NY 13208-1766
Phone: (315) 471-6762

Rosary Monastery
St. Ann's Road, Port of Spain
TRINIDAD, WEST INDIES
Phone: (868) 624-7648

Mother of God Monastery
1430 Riverdale Street
West Springfield, MA 01089-4698
Phone: (413) 736-3639
Web: www.op-stjoseph.org/nuns/ws/index.htm
Email: monasteryws@aol.com

Made in the USA
Lexington, KY
07 June 2018